the horse that *broke* two legs

& *survived*

A transformative true story
from trauma to freedom

Zoë Coade

Published by
Zoë Coade, the Netherlands

Contact via website:
www.thehorsethatbroketwolegs.com
www.facebook.com/thehorsethatbroketwolegs

© Cover artwork by Zoë Coade
© Cover digitalised by atelier moreno

First edition, reprint November 2017
ISBN-978-90-826145-0-3 (paperback)
ISBN-978-90-826145-1-0 (e-Book)
ISBN 978-90-826145-2-7 (Dutch paperback)
ISBN 978-90-826145-3-4 (German paperback)

Please visit this book's companion website and social media page for images, videos and updates:

www.thehorsethatbroketwolegs.com
www.facebook.com/thehorsethatbroketwolegs

ACKNOWLEDGEMENTS

To all that genuinely cared, supported, loved, laughed and cried with us when the light at the end of the tunnel faded, to the day it shone bright once again and to everyone that has touched our life in one way or another.
We are very blessed to say there are so many of you. I never knew such kindness both during and after her accident, in no particular order:

First three month carers: Gemma Avezaat, Geert Blijham, Anneke van Brakel, Mariska Romkes, Liesbeth Hoogkamer, Micha Henker, Hanneke Vosse, Jolanda Nachtegeller, Jacqueline Lentz, Galina van Lieshout-Peeters, Annette Flottmann-Nilsson, Diana Luyten, Annette vd Berg, Kika de Leon, Cassie Tooms and everybody that stopped by and said hello.
Long term recovery home: Marieke Molenaar and Eddy Modde.
Long term recovery guardian angel: Marieke van den Worm.
Current farm owner and boarder: Rutger van der Peet.
Equine doctor: Hans Coster and all the staff at Paardendokters.
Equine dietary advice: Rene Wielens.
Hoof care and dietary advice: Annette Nielsen.
Blacksmith and special shoes: Kees van Bijnen.
Long term recovery hoof care: Petra van Langevelde.
Osteopathy aftercare: Annemarijn Laan.
Massage Therapy aftercare: Marieke Looysen.
Equine dentist: Marielle Heuvelman.
Life coach and best friend: Carrie Neeves.
Advisor and friend: Amanda Watkins.
Present day share and care: Amber Schoonderwoerd, Galina van Lieshout-Peeters and Dieuwertje Rutten.
Present day vacation care: Mirjam Spitzers, Anouk Boer, Mariska Romkes, Claire Visser, Katinka Postma, Lonneke Rutten, Amber Schoonderwoerd, Galina van Lieshout-Peeters and Dieuwertje Rutten.
Website assistance: Werner Reuser.

My mentors: Silke Vallentin, Kristi Smith, Michael Wanzenried, Joyce Mulder, Romi Eikendal, Therese Chouchene & Greetje Hackvoort.
Proof readers: Liam Coade, Mike Coade, Amber Schoonderwoerd, Carrie Neeves, Jort van Kruiningen, Mirjam Spitzers and Roos Koole.
Last minute.com inspiration: Angie C Baily and Chris Wood.
Final proof read and edit: Sarah Carr

DEDICATIONS

For my parents Brenda and Mike and my brother Michael who gave me the opportunity to be around horses from a very young age, my love for horses is understood by no-other.
Thank you and love you.

For my god-daughter Millicent Kay Cox, may you and your big brother Alexander grow up to be strong, independent and whoever you want to be.
Always be inspired.

For my friends who are often in my thoughts: Sarah Cox, Anthony Burpitt, Jan Cox, Melanie Ramos, Sue Keefe, Kate Willett and Pascale Mooij.

Lastly for my husband Jort, somebody in this lifetime I am very fortunate to have met; it is my version of heaven, to be with you.

In memory:
Esther Coade, Ilo Mae Isabelle Swaby
and Tineke van Kruiningen-Bonder.

I love you. Every day.

FRONT COVER

The childlike black horse emblem can be found in
Japan in a city called Mima美馬.
Historically a home to horse breeders, the name is derived from
two Japanese characters meaning *beautiful horse.*

CONTENTS

CHAPTER 1   Part I

Mima 美馬   The beautiful black horse

*'La señora **mima** su hijo demasiado' – 'The lady spoils her child'. Spanish translates as: 'To give a lot of affection or too much attention'. Used in both a positive or negative way.*

What a beautiful horse were my thoughts when I saw her for the first time. It was the end of May in the year of 2000, I was twenty five and she was just two weeks old. She was not to be my first horse; I had the pleasure of owning quite a few before her, all of which had been formerly named. I searched hard for a name that depicted sincerely what I thought she was and beautiful-horse translated in Japanese is pronounced Me-ma. Therefore, for the first nine months of her life that was to be her name. She was everything I dreamed of, with a dark brown almost black shiny coat and fluffy blonde wisps of baby hair blended into the tips of her ears, nose and legs. With no other distinct markings, her big brown eyes would stare back at me with an amicable silence. She was also very big, by far outsizing her siblings and by two months of age was almost too tall to reach under her mother to drink her milk. Her sire, (a name given to a horse's father), was a pure English Thoroughbred and her dam, the mother, was an Irish Draft. The combination of both breeds can create a very strong, athletic and charismatic breed known and registered in Great Britain and Ireland as an Irish Sports Horse, or an Irish Hunter.

Mima
The name Mima never stuck, and was replaced with what I thought was both pretty and equally significant, and that was

Mia. In Italian it's famously known meaning is *mine* and one could relish the thought that this was indeed my intention, the reverse being I think that in the end, I simply preferred that name.

At four months of age she was weaned from her dam and turned free to live with the other weanlings. They were bred from the same sire all of which were at least two months older than Mia, making her the youngest. Some would argue she was fairly premature to be taken from her dam, I am sure the situation was just easier for the owner to wean them all at once since it was a traditional breeding stud farm and a business. It is done that way sometimes and the horses can still turn out alright if they are weaned considerately. In the wild it is also known for mares to push away their young prematurely, this is one of those questions we will probably never really know the answer as to why, mostly we would assume the mare's decision was not without calculation. One benefit here was that she was weaned fairly and by that I mean relatively stress free, and thankfully not having been put in a situation where she was left alone like many young horses can be; you can only imagine the unnecessary trauma.

Amidst a valley of green hills in the heart of Great Britain the young foals had access to ad lib hay under the protection of a large corrugated iron barn with fresh water and approximately one acre of fair grassland. It was not too bad a start at life really, and without a dam or adult herd members to teach and defend her, she learned from this young age as horses can, the instant meaning of ultimate survival: how to perfectly and with absolute precision deliver a kick at a moment's decision, and how to accurately bite with enough intention that it can leave the recipient with missing hair, of which sometimes the remnants can be found in the donor's teeth.

These facts are not here to instil that Mia or any horse for that matter are monsters, far from it. My wish in this first chapter is to give some insight and understanding of the horse and their language, so the value of this story reaches the reader with a deeper level of sentiment, and in particular the path of this one horse. What is explicitly special is the keyhole vision I will provide from her early life to present day, and the explanation of why I think certain behaviours turned out the way they did, and how particular characteristics developed. It is quite the account and leads directly to the story of how she broke two limbs and survived.

CHAPTER 1   Part II

The Equus   Their language briefly explained

Studying the equine species, their behaviour and language for many people like me is a full time commitment and a lifetime study, because quite simply there is so much to learn. As dedicated as I am and as disciplined as I can be, I am happy to admit I will never know it all. I will also never compare myself to the real masters of this trade in the past or the present; it is actually not worth it. I have heard one of my mentor's quotes a few times now that says:

"You can fool the fans, but you cannot fool the players!"

The word *players* does not just mean just the masters or well educated equine enthusiasts, but also the horses themselves. If we are to talk about trainers and instructors who offer their services to teach and train humans and horses, it should be recognised that credentials and education are not a specific proof that they are good at it. I mention this here because for myself and many people around the globe, the most fascinating part of this process and the representation of what a true horseman or horsewoman really is, is nothing less than a one hundred and ten percent commitment, and some sort of shift in your way of thinking. Unless some of the following things come naturally to a person, it can make the job more challenging. Not impossible, just more challenging.

In no particular order these qualities are: accepting the horse's nature and not fighting it, being excellent at what you do from start to finish, facilitating skills, habits and techniques to a level of mastery, knowing when to and when not to use ego, learning not to repeat unwanted behaviours, being capable of remaining calm in high stress situations, having a high belief system driven and maintained through motivation, an ability and flexibility to adapt to all situations, an unquestionable compassion and empathy, a capacity to listen and observe without judgment, an ability to set personal emotions and goals aside, and in most cases, knowing the why and not just the how of what one is doing, a life experienced with and without horses, an ability to say no and mean it, and lastly to have faith in one's self, because if you do not, the customer and/or horse certainly will not. I have yet to know personally someone who carries all of these attributes naturally, but I know people who do have them and have worked incredibly hard for it, and those are the people I look up to, they are my mentors and masters.

In my teachings I have been known to refer to our dear friend the horse anthropomorphically and jokingly of course as a type of sociopath or psychopath, and although it is not always ideal to use human characteristics as a comparison, during an explanation it can oftentimes help one's client during coaching find some sort of level ground. Personally and in short, if horses were humans, I do not think we would like them very much; as a matter of fact we would probably lock them up and quite literally throw away the key.
You might ask why and my response would be something along the lines of explaining the horse's brain, which by the way is no bigger than the size of a large orange; such a large animal and yet such a small brain. Biologically there is not much room in there for laughter, tears, lies, worrying about yesterday, tomorrow or the next pay cheque. They just do not think like us, period. It is physically not possible, because that part of the brain where we do all that kind of thinking does not exist in theirs. Yet what they do have is incredibly interesting and for fun I often wonder what it would be like if we could somehow climb into their body, feel their mind and see the world through their eyes.

In shock, we would probably exit immediately because it would feel so alien to us.
So why compare them to a sociopath?

It is nothing to be alarmed about if you think of it like this: in a social environment for horses, which thankfully is becoming more and more popular this century, they absolutely want to, need to and do communicate with each other and one of the ways they do this is by using physical play and dominance. Again to keep this very simple, they will either play fight or they will really fight. Two of those known ways of fighting are biting or kicking, and sometimes both at the same time. The point is if you are around them long enough and they are fortunate enough to live in a social environment, at some point you will see a horse have a confrontation and kick another horse hard, and I mean very hard, maybe two, even three times and in some cases will even cause bleeding.
The interesting part is that when they have finished, you will not see the dominating equine stand there afterwards with a sad look on their face apologising for what they have just done, it does not happen like that.
People might humanize this and swear that their horse was sorry for certain things, but if we look at the biological makeup of the horse it is actually not built into their system to do so; survival is in their system and outsmarting predators is in their system, saying sorry is not. Another important fact is that horses outsmart humans all of the time, it is what they are designed to do: outsmart predators and outsmart us.

With humour in my thoughts, I have to giggle at the comedy value of exactly what they can do to do just that. Again if you have been around them long enough, you will at some point see an uneducated horse drag its human to an anonymous bucket of grain or towards lush grass, or take their human for a walk, usually where they are not supposed to go. These are the kind of games they can and will play and yes it can be quite dangerous, especially since they are a living, breathing decision making

animal. The empathetic solution to resolve these issues while preserving the dignity of the horse does not have to be violent either, and we know this now with today's technology and the profound information available, so let's change that.
So what is abnormal in a sociopath's psychology compared to someone who is not?

Typically they are known to have little if any feeling of remorse, little if any empathy or regret, the same goes for guilt, and the real shocker is: *neither does a horse!*

Please do not be mistaken, I am not saying that a horse does not feel or have any emotions; they most definitely have feelings for both long and short term intervals. Some examples of these can be things like verbally calling in distress, forms of depression, anxiousness, mourning and sadness, peaks of happiness, bouts of adrenaline, peacefulness, fear and even momentary anger. What we must not forget is that it is dissimilar to a human's emotions, it can look and might even feel the same but it is different.
On behalf of perhaps most horse lovers, I am sincerely sorry to disappoint the non-equestrian reader when revealing a common place where this is often misguided, and that is on the big screen. The real truth is that any footage where horses are shown to constantly neigh or whinny and make friendly vocal sounds towards each other or their human companion is extremely fictitious. Most of the time a horse will only use his voice when he is emotional, afraid or both and that is usually by calling for the safety of herd members whether they live together, or not. Another example is when they are in the habit of demanding food from their humans. With this in mind, one could question what it would be like if horses were indeed so vocal to their humans, as it is shown in these works of fiction:
Would we treat them any differently?
I think the answer would be *yes*.

What we do know is that when a horse is young, a dam will communicate vocally and depending on its environment it will vary in quantity, and as the foal matures and becomes more independent this diminishes. A very silent world compared to ours, enchanting too, and it is because of this a horse that spends energy to greet you for example at the gate with the added bonus of a whinny really is one of the most amazing feelings in the world. Procured from a few situations really, like the human having an excellent bond with the horse or being the conveyor of a daily routine or a bearer of regular food, it can also be a combination of all three. Let us never forget it is all about survival for them and as a result there is of course a flipside, and that is where humans are only too aware of the injuries they can inflict on themselves and each other. Therefore they will submit these remarkable animals to confinement and worse still isolation.

This is a subject I feel adamant about and will briefly make some justifiable points. Housing a horse in a stable is neither a good thing nor a bad thing; to me personally it just really depends on how it is used, how often and for how long. If a horse is a valued individual especially for things like sport, breeding or to protect a high status, unless they really do not have a choice, I do not care what anyone says. Being locked away for some twenty plus hours a day for years on end is certainly not for the love of a horse's true wellbeing, mental and emotional needs. It is for the human's needs and human's needs only.

A bit harsh? Yes.

Unfair? I would not say so.

I am not proclaiming that a stable, or box as it can often be referred to is a bad place, but for a social and athletic flight animal that is designed to move, who does not have a choice of freedom because they are locked up, it can be sugar coated however you like, you will never convince me that it is not a prison. Not just to their psychology, but also to their physiology and if we are really honest, it is only accepted in society because a horse cannot complain verbally or cry in a way that is recognised as desperate or abusive. Domestic animals like a dog or a cat can and will verbally cry in such a way it reaches the human's emotions directly. The difference is that horses complain too but mostly in silence, what you might not hear you can learn to see, if you look hard enough.

 It raises another question again, what if horses did communicate more verbally like they do in the movies?

Could we get away with it?

I think the answer would be *no*.

As mentioned, and without trying to sound sanctimonious I do not have anything against them either because stabling horses can have its benefits. An ideal condition that a horse can cope with quite well is something like using a box part-time with the opportunity to go outside onto a decent piece of acreage where they really can move around, frolic and play. Too often I see this opportunity given yet the paddock is poor or very small, or they have too little time outside. However realistically I am aware this is not always possible, so for the horse's sake can only hope at some point in their life they are moved to somewhere else where these options are available.

There are so many pros and cons, but the reason I like to use a stable when and where possible is to verify some things in my horse's lives too. They have to live in this world, a world that is shrinking around all of us; the land is fast becoming less available especially in Europe. Nobody can predict what could happen tomorrow and one day we may well have no choice but to keep them in a stable.

The way I see it is that I want my horses to be adaptable to all living arrangements and to also be comfortable with them. If for example I travel to a clinic or demonstration where we have to stay at least one night, the most frequent option of temporary accommodation for a horse is indeed a stable. Sure I could tell the organisers I am not coming because I insist my horse must be in a paddock outside, or I can be comforted that they will have the stable for a few days or longer, simply because of its educational value.

I know some readers will question the latter, but the point is in general I think it helps a horse with life experience like standing in a trailer for long periods while travelling. It can give one peace of mind because it is not new to them if they were subject to an injury or illness, which in return required rest or isolation. There is a big chance that the stress is reduced and they will have a better chance of coping. I just do not believe in confining them or any animal actually to an eternity of a life inside four walls.

By her nature and from a very young age, Mia was what you would typically refer to in the horse game, as top-in-rank and her siblings of both sexes were living at the mercy of this strong and consistent alpha mare. We must give some credit to the beauty of Mother Nature and her extraordinary gift of instinct, the young filly acted as a replacement adult herd member and maintained their discipline. She fell a bit short on that deal because nobody actually disciplined her, later in life they tried; we will get to that shortly.

The equus family are amazing animals, they have the ability to adapt and learn constantly from the moment they arrive on earth to the day they leave. Because they are not like you and I, and they are full faculty learners at birth, known in biological terms as a precocial species. A great way of explaining it is perhaps using an example like the old saying:
You cannot teach an old dog a new trick.
Just like us, dogs get older and their biological brain function simply deteriorates; that is because they are a predator. Whereas a horse's brain will usually continue to function at the same learning capacity when they are old as when they were young, because of this ingenious requirement to learn and survive, and that is simply because they are a prey animal. It can feel like a young horse is learning faster than an adult horse simply because they do not know anything yet.

The equine family also have what I like to refer to as the three super sensory systems, and these are their ears, eyes and nose.

Without going too deeply into how they actually function I will briefly explain their advantages and some informative details. A horse has excellent hearing and will often use it before they use their sight, or they can and will combine hearing and sight. Their vison is excellent, suitable for their lifestyle as a prey animal and in comparison to ours it is by far more advanced. Then there is smell, they can use it to determine safety in the air but will mostly use it to smell each other, food, objects etc.

With this brief knowledge we can quickly conclude what a relaxed and contented horse looks like. It would be one whose head is hung low with its ears lying still and barely detecting sounds. Their eyes are soft, almost closing with relaxation and their breathing is very shallow, almost to the point where sometimes it is hard to see their nostrils move with each breath. An unrelaxed horse will have its head up high and its ears will be darting backwards or forwards, searching for something scary or for safety. Or, they will be transfixed on something they have identified as a possible or definite danger, followed by flaring nostrils trying to breathe and fill the lungs with as much oxygen as possible in preparation to run.

This is incredibly important to understand simply because when a horse is happy or content they are for the most part as mentioned earlier, silent. In fear they might snort and when feeling lost or alone they might call out in distress, but for the most part there is no vocal sound. It is also vital to understand that a horse can isolate sound, vison and smell; this means they can have one sound coming in one ear and another in the other. They can isolate their vison and they can isolate their smell, it is quite remarkable and might also explain why they have been on the planet for some 55 million years and mankind as we know it, a mediocre 200 thousand years in comparison.

Some further interesting points are that when both of a horse's ears are forwards; it simply means his focus is forwards, it does not mean he is happy. As a matter of fact and out of choice, when a horse uses both ears focused forwards combined with his eyes it means he is generally looking that way or he is observing whether there is danger or not. There is a great confusion and disillusion that a horse is only happy when his ears are forwards. Naturally when people take photos of their horses they want the picture to be nice and in doing so will go to great lengths to get the horse to put its ears forward. During photoshoots they are asking an animal who does not smile with its ears forwards, to do something which is unnatural to them and sometimes for hours. When in fact what they are doing is asking the horse to use a survival reflex and then stand still, relax and behave. I hope you can see the significant message here, it is not intended to criticise it is intended to educate. With that said I would love to see a change in this in the equine world where there are more pictures of horses standing content with relaxed ears and soft eyes and more true to their form and nature and not true to the idealism of a humans benefit or ego.

For Mia at this young age, she knew who she was and what she needed to do in order to get priority over food and water; and what I am about to tell you is also the origin of how she learned and accomplished the art of outsmarting humans, especially predictable ones. The beautiful little two week old filly that I had put a handshake deposit on was in fact wild, meaning she was never touched by a human. Out of all the stock for sale she was by far the strongest and although being the youngest, was the only one that had some form of stamina, a shiny coat and of course cost quite a few pounds more than the other foals available for purchase. In my excitement at the prospect of my next dream horse I literally pointed her out of the herd and said *that one,* shook hands with the seller and paid the deposit. Between that day and when she could come home with me seven months later, I visited her about every three weeks and although with each visit she grew more confident about having humans around, I could not actually touch her.

It was a funny situation, although she was partly mine because I had paid a deposit I never felt comfortable enough to step in and train or tame her without full ownership. I will quite literally and for the rest of my life never forget the day she could come home,

I felt sick with excitement and anxiety because she was after all wild and untamed, and I hoped in my deepest hope of hopes that there had been some change in her experience of humans since my last and final visit a few weeks before.

Deep down I knew of course this was not going to be, it had not been communicated to me that the seller would do this. For a moment my concerns were lifted, the man with whom I made the purchase slowly and apparently without issue led Mia out of the barn away from her herd, towards the big green horse lorry I had hired to get her home. The question of how he got her head collar on has never been answered, she was very quiet and in hindsight I am pretty sure she was shell shocked having never left the safety of the farm or her herd before, and was at that moment in time being taken to some unknown place. Her eyes clearly expressed her thoughts, showing the white membrane like a rabbit in the headlights of a car and I remember telling myself: *It will be fine when I get her home, let's just get her home.*

Well of course he did try to lead her up the ramp and into the back of the lorry and not knowing really what he was asking of her; she planted her feet and naturally said no. She did not fight, she just froze. Without really thinking about it and as if he had done this a hundred times before, he quite literally said to me:

"Are you ready?"

I nodded, half in disbelief as to what was about to happen, yet my body was already reacting to what I could not believe was about to happen. He simply put his arms around her like you would a young calf, picked her up and walked up the ramp; one can only assume he must have used all of his strength to then set her down in the back of the lorry. My subconscious reaction to his unspoken gesture was to close the gate, which I did. He then looked at me, shook my hand one final time and muttered some awkward kind of farewell walking off to never to be seen again. I think I must have looked like someone just stole my mother and after a quick shake of our heads and a much needed comforting chat with my accomplice to get over the initial shock, I was thankful she had landed on all four feet. It had begun and I was extremely pleased she was in the lorry. In my excitement I could not wait to get her home and start this new friendship by offering her tons of love and education.

CHAPTER 1   Part III

Bonding   How we began

Bond: two or more individuals who become
temporarily or permanently, emotionally attached.

I scheduled the week off work to spend time with my new best
friend, and believe me when I say I would do things very
differently today if I had known then what I know now. I
purchased a special halter, one that did not have metal or plastic
buckles but Velcro instead, with the intention that I could keep it
on in the stable so I could at least start to handle her. That way if
she ever got her head entangled it would merely pull off; at the
time I thought this was genius and to some extent still do today.
Before she was allowed out on the land with the other horses, she
had to be de-wormed and vaccinated first, thus allowing us more
one-to-one time. It was not a bad idea really since I had no idea
how I would have caught her if she could go out on the huge
pastures. I spent hours upon hours sitting in the stable allowing
her to touch me and when the moment felt right I touched her,
another example of when a stable can be a handy place. This
went rather well and although I did not know it then, I think the
reason the taming process towards me worked so quickly was
because she was given the choice to touch and investigate me
first.
Before long I could touch her all over and could even lead her
out of the barn area for a curious walk and exercise. I also started
the process of teaching her how to tie and stand in one place, and
how to lift her legs to clean the underside of her hooves. Pretty
traditional stuff really having never tamed a wild horse before;
there were many things going on that I did not realise until much

26

later. She had started to teach me extraordinary things, things that I had never learned in the past with other horses and I believe this was the very beginning of my journey, learning not just how to look at horses and how to train them, but also how to really listen to them. She taught me that, because I was the hand that fed her and because I had allowed her to make the first meaningful contact, that steadfast with all her heart she knew I was very safe and if anybody tried to interfere with our herd of two, she would soon let them know about it. At first and in a subtle way she actually dominated me, and later this did change, getting much worse before it got better. At this particular point in time her thoughts of other humans were incredibly insecure. One minute she could be in flight mode and be very spooky and afraid, and the next in fight mode and explode into an act of self-defence. Something which as the years passed gave her names, like *mad mare* and *naughty horse*.

The one I remember the most was when someone said:

"That bitch of a horse is wild."

In hindsight the funny thing was they were so right, minus the bitch part of course. She was indeed still wild, tame only to the thoughts, association or perhaps notion of food and water, a routine and maybe me.

I say maybe me because if she really trusted me *would she still have acted the same way?*

Back then I would have said *no*, today I would say *it depends*.

I have further evaluations of how I think this cocooned into what it did and for lack of better words became an extremely unhandy part of our life together. For many years this behaviour continued and eventually to the point it almost cost me her life.

One of the primary ingredients contributing to her sensitive response towards humans happened during the week of taming, after I finally got her home. It must have been the second or third day she was home and the vet had to visit and give her a vaccine shot and her microchip against theft, she was of course still genuinely wild of some sorts. I would not say she was super afraid when they were hanging around, she was bravely showing signs of curiosity with her nose but she was certainly difficult to handle when somebody else tried to touch her, and of course she was learning how to use her strength against them successfully and very quickly by wiggling her body away like a giant worm with legs. At this time I could at least feel she trusted me to some extent, welcoming some relief in my concerns. This was because she had started the process of bonding with me long before I had realised.

 I remember leading her out of the stable which was inside a big long barn, waiting for the vet and his assistant to do their thing in the corridor. Mia was again quiet at first glance; the vet was quick to prepare his needle, clean her neck with an alcohol swab and inject the needle and its contents into the allocated neck muscle. She protested a little, like most horses can and some humans might, but seemed okay. Of course she was not; next came the same routine, and how quickly she could resonate with the humans' predictability astounded me. She knew whatever he was going to do next was going to hurt just as much, if not more than the last time, and her answer naturally in horse language was to rear up on her hind legs and try her hardest to get away. But, being the humans we were at that moment in time and with the knowledge we had, all three of us held on for dear life and before you knew it he had managed to shoot her in the neck; except this time with the microchip dispenser, which by the way looked very much like a gun. It was over, and Mia who was momentarily agitated huddled close to my side. After a quick chat with the vet I led her to her stable where she continued to eat her hay and remain quiet, as though nothing had happened.

The big day finally arrived where she was allowed to go out on the pasture with some other horses. I was extremely happy for her and still slightly concerned that I might not be able to catch her. Figuring we would approach that problem if and when it happened, she was set free to run and play on the beautiful and hilly pastures. In those days you could choose to have your horse twelve hours in a stable and twelve hours outside, I never had a problem catching her.

For most of my life directly after leaving school and also after we immigrated to the Netherlands, I have worked a full time job.

To take care of my horses I would always arrive before the birds sang every morning and long after they had gone to bed most nights. I love the process of caring for horses and back then I did not ask for help often. Mia made good friends with a young horse and a retired pony, they were however definitely lower in her rank and although I never recall seeing her actively play, even to the present day, they sure ran a lot and never left her side. She was not particularly nice to them, but then what is nice in horse language? She was not what I would call mean either, with only the odd kick or bite here and there, no real hair removing moments. It is the same to this day really where her herd members have changed, but not her attitude. She stayed with that group for about fourteen months and as you can imagine she was getting incredibly big and tall. It was, and still is, a beautiful farm where there are some traditional rules like separating sexes and I was informed it was time to introduce her to the big girls' field.

We'd had some quite terrible weather so the clay ground which covered that area was incredibly slippery from the rain, it concerned me some. However rules were rules and I turned her lose in her new habitat to meet her new herd. A small habit of hers was and still is that once I turn her loose, she will walk about eight or ten meters and then run off like a fire cracker as if suddenly appreciating she is free. She did the same this day except of course it was a new field and there were new horses. These horses were big and some even towered over her not-so-small self. There were different breeds varying from cold bloods to warmbloods, and with their hierarchy under threat they came straight over to see who the latest recruit was. Just as Mia had settled to eat some grass, a big warmblood galloped over first and almost at full speed, it was the alpha-mare. As she approached, she executed a sliding stop, turned on a sixpence and double barrelled Mia with both her hind legs about three or four times before galloping off, only to return with a friend who also helped do the same thing again. I remember thinking:

"Shit, that's probably another vet bill."

The irony is that she was not hurt, perhaps bruised, reduced some by the protection of her blanket from the sharp angle of their hooves. It was how Mia reacted to these interactions that fascinated me the most, she just took the blows and by that I mean she literally did not move, it was as if she was made of steel, and once they had finished and moved out of her bubble she continued to eat.
I saw no signs of nervousness; she was not calling for her now ex-buddies in the old field, it was as if she simply knew again that that was where she was supposed to be and only cared about the food and eventually the water. She blew away both my mind, and the minds of the embarrassed but sympathetic owners of the dominating horses. They had come to watch the circus, something quite common when introducing a new herd member.

Maybe fifteen minutes or so passed and during that time the rest of the herd had come over to investigate. I think there were twelve or so mares, and around eight of those including the alpha mare and her accomplice got in close to do the usual smelling of the nose, followed by the odd squeal and kick. It did not take long before they all had their heads down and were eating the grass with Mia right in the middle, it was done. I never saw the mares pick on her again and in fact do remember sometimes squinting in my efforts to not be too concerned, when I saw Mia take unusual action and use her energy to validate her status, for indeed she had become the alpha again and without much effort in this new herd.

Another contributing factor towards her behaviours happened when she was around two years old. She was as usual out in the field, and when she came in I discovered a puncture wound high up on the outside of her foreleg, smack bang in the middle of the common digital extensor muscle, an important muscle at that. There was not too much blood visible but there was a big unwelcome gaping hole. Naturally I called the vet and he gave me the usual medical prescription you would have expected in those days for that type of injury. I was instructed to flush the wound three times a day to keep it clean with particular products. I will mention here, a practice not much different to today except for perhaps the prescribed medications and cleaning agents. The best way for this type of wound to heal is in fact from inside to outside, which amongst other things can help prevent infections and reduce scar tissue.

I did as instructed, making sure the wound did not close and taking her temperature as much as possible. On the third day her temperature was exceptionally high, I do not remember the number I just know it was very high. I called the vet and they said to give it a few hours, and if there was no change that morning they would make an emergency visit by lunch time. Regrettably it did not change and by then she had also stopped eating and drinking, I was terrified. The vet came, a woman this time and told me it looked like she had a severe infection and that I needed to get her to the clinic as soon as possible. I was shocked, how could a simple puncture wound cause so much commotion.

Using my trailer I managed to get her to the clinic and I remember being a bit short tempered with the vet. I wanted to know whether they could have told me to do something differently to prevent this from happening; I had been meticulous in my efforts. Of course this was not possible; they had given their best diagnosis with the knowledge they had and in hindsight said it was quite possible the wound was contaminated.

With huge reluctance and pain in my heart, I left her at the veterinary practice in their care and headed straight to the barn to search the pasture one last time for the perpetrator that could do such harm. I was convinced there was absolutely nothing she could have cut herself on in that way until I found it. Slapping myself on the forehead I realised it was the corner edge of the water tank which carried some rust. I also found small evidence of watery blood running down its side. I was kind of relieved to know what it could be, but also angry at myself for not finding it sooner. As I called the vet to give the new evidence, the owner of the property fired up his tractor with rasp in hand to file down the edges of all the water tanks in the pastures. The next day it was confirmed she had sepsis and she would have to stay at the clinic for at least a week, maybe longer depending on her recovery. The fact that she was not eating or drinking was also a high concern. I was very upset and took extra days off work so I could visit her as much as possible, nothing else mattered. The interesting development of all of this was that on the second or third day of her admittance, I can't quite remember for sure, she started to eat out of my hand and when I left she ate nothing. Thankfully her temperature dropped to normal values around the fourth day and her survival instinct was strong, telling her to eat and drink again. The imbalance of this situation and with great sadness was how Mia perceived her treatment; unfortunately it was already too late. That first experience of her vaccine and microchip and now this had left a scar, a very deep one. Each day she had to have medications administered via several types of needle entry, one for a drip to keep her hydrated, others for antibiotics and all kinds of things really, she was like a pin cushion. She of course did not know it was for her own good and each and every time they had to inject her she protested just that bit more. In the end when I could finally bring her home after cleverly prescribing me oral medications for her post care the vet nurse advised me:

"Some discipline would not go amiss and if she were my horse she would soon be shown who the boss is!"

I remember nodding *yes* to politely indicate she was right yet inside I was thinking something like:

"Oh piss off; I don't have these problems, only you do!"

It was another situation where I could not wait to get her home and away from the big misunderstanding world. Surprisingly both to and from the veterinary clinic she walked into the trailer like a pro, I think she was just too weak to say no even if she wanted to, and her food source and saviour had once again returned.

My general training was conventionally adapted to the requirements of her age, some things we had going quite nicely without much issue, and other things the complete opposite, that being mostly other people. Her second and third vaccinations were interesting to say the least; the same male doctor administered the second vaccination six weeks after the initial one. It went not much different to the first time with her wiggling and protesting, and then again by somebody else a year later. The annual vaccination was met with some different tactics and the vet in attendance was female. I told her the problems we had discovered in the past which she did not seem too concerned about, and quickly decided she was not going to inject her in the neck muscle but instead into the breast muscle just above and in-between the front legs. My goodness if she was not fast and just like before, the alcohol swab came out, Mia already new that smell of course. She pinned back her ears in warning and shuffled around with all her frustrations aimed only at the vet resulting of course in her not being able to touch her at all, so with no other options to offer it was a case of hit or miss. She did hit the mark; except she had used a technique where they put the hypodermic needle head in first so they can connect the syringe containing the injectable fluid after, once the horse has settled; quite a common practice used for large animals. I hoped it would work too actually but man it just got worse, Mia protested to the point I started to get very nervous for her safety. It did not help that the vet became short in temper; the whole thing was a mess. Finally the vet asked:

"How is she if you touch her?"

I responded with my arms aching at holding the four hundred kilos together:

"I don't know, let's give it a try!"

The true fact is I did not know how she would react; the horse was fighting for her life with a sharp object sticking out of her chest. Fortunately the vet did at least back away and out of her bubble in a bid to help my efforts to calm her. I recall taking a deep breath, clearing my mind of any negative thoughts and telling her with every cell in brain and body to trust me. To our delight she started to settle and only with a ticklish response let me touch the needle, I looked over my shoulder towards the vet bursting with pride, she handed me the syringe which I connected to the needle and injected the fluid. From that day forth and continuing for many years to come, I gave her the annual vaccinations myself. Foolishly in my ignorance I really did not think it was a bad thing, that I could do everything with this horse and others could not, I was so incredibly and stupidly wrong.

It was actually my first lesson, although I did not grasp it then, that a human's attitude was part of the key to this horse's heart. Such a big horse that will display a fight mode, which we must not forget is because it is afraid or unsure, can create a nervous human. Therefore it can also create an unfortunate rebound effect. Since the horse does not have the logic to resolve the issue it would then only be up to the human to change his primary human response, when working with animals who act this way it is common practice to become volatile and impatient, or worse still violent. I had not witnessed anybody be violent towards her, I would not have allowed that anyway, but the human's attitude was already enough. They did not have to hurt her; she just knew they did not like her, especially when they were angry.

CHAPTER 2   Part I

The awakening   A serious problem

It was around the beginning of 2003 when she was three years old that it dawned on me, I needed some serious help. I knew I did not want physical help, not yet anyway. The knowledge and experience I had in those days told me instinctively that violence or forms of breaking her spirit would be the common answer for the problems she had, and that was not welcome in my *horse-hold*. For this reason I searched for something else, the world was making such huge and evolutionary changes, I knew there had to be another way I could help her, I just did not know how yet.

A magazine which I had on subscription grabbed my curiosity, by landing with a louder thump than usual on the doormat. I had to see what it was, and there wrapped in clear plastic with the magazine was a DVD, the contents of which were exactly what I had been looking for. I had always been a big fan of the book: The Horse Whisperer by Nicolas Evans, and to this day must have read it at least ten times. I lost count of how many times I watched the movie, I even wrote parts of this book listening to the Motion picture Soundtrack by Thomas Newman. Somewhere in my unconscious consciousness, I had hoped that this cowboy who helped troubled horses would be real.
In my research I was delighted to find out he certainly was, and there were many of them. But this time it was real where I was standing and not in some romantic notion of every horsey girls dream, being an idyllic ranch in the Western Hemisphere or so far away he may as well not exist. From the moment I opened the plastic sleeve to the very same evening when I sat down to watch the video, was the very beginning of who Mia and I are

today. Having already started to listen to my horse unwarily, I was now for the first time in my life, really ready to learn about her and had the tools at hand to do so. I was excited to learn too, especially since it meant learning about the one thing I have loved with my entire heart, ever since I could first make decisions for myself: the beautiful horses. It was from here onwards that learning also became an addiction. At school I was your average student with not many grade A's in my portfolio. I think it was because none of the subjects interested me, except maybe sports and art, you could say just the fun stuff! Somehow the horses would always take over or be an excuse for my inaptness, I actually turned down playing national field hockey because I wanted to do pony gymkhanas instead. The humour about this was that I was quite brilliant at hockey and I really sucked at the gymkhanas.

One of the first times the realisation had set in that we did indeed have a very serious problem was about four months before I received the DVD. A big project came up at work which meant for a while I had to do extra-long hours both during the week and at weekends, therefore my daily ritual of being my horse's sole carer morning and night was temporarily broken. Vacation time was no issue, it was usually summertime when I planned to go away anyway and later that same year, some issues with both her back legs gave me permission to let her out on the land twenty four hours a day, something I will get back to in this chapter. There was a nice young girl who worked for extra money taking horses to and from the fields and who also did small chores for you like changing blankets and mucking out your stable for a reasonable fee, it was perfect solution. I thought that I would just ask for her help and all would be well, or so I had hoped. I had arranged for her to take Mia to the field in the morning and muck out my stable and if I could not get there in the evening I would call and let her know. The girl was very kind and sweet and after having a chat and explaining that Mia could be:
"Well, erm, difficult!"

36

She reassured me it was going to be fine and that she was probably no match compared to some of the horses she had the pleasure of working with.

Being content with her confidence, I did not think much more of it. On the first long work day I could make it to the barn that evening, I was happy as I had already arrived at work that morning three hours earlier than usual. The girl said:

"She was easy in the stable but I had to put a halter on to change her blankets, she was a bit flighty on her way to the field, other than that no problem!"

It was done, I could work and not worry. The weeks passed and if I remember correctly I forgot to tell her when I could be there in the mornings again, and on the un-mentioned morning I had arrived in time to see her lead Mia out of the barn towards the field. My jaw dropped so quickly it should have broken, how could I have been so naïve, of course the girl said it was fine, of course she ignored the pushing, biting and head butts and of course she somehow got her to the field, of course, of course, of course, because for a lot of people and still today these behaviours are accepted as normal. It was not her job to train my horse.

She had admitted that Mia wore bigger boots than most of the horses she had to handle but it did not deter her, actually she was quite brilliant. I saw the tail end of Mia jumping and leaping all over the place, thankfully the girl was walking as calm as she could next to her. However if it was not for a moment's glimpse I would have missed it. At one point Mia turned her head and I could see very clearly that the girl held her under the chin as tightly as possible, but what really made my heart skip a beat was the chain over her nose. Neither the girl nor Mia saw me until she started to walk back to the barn from the field. Somehow in this short moment I managed to get myself together and passively I told her of my mistake for forgetting to let her know I would be there from now on, that I would contact her if we needed her again, I thanked her and went on my way. I did not say anything, I did not communicate in any way that I did not like what I saw, because it was simply the way it was and the way it was done; I also had no solution to offer any of us at that time.

What also hurt and niggled my stomach was the realisation that all the horses I had owned in the past were a gift from the gods. They were sweet, easy, bomb proof, with the odd bite maybe but never a horse with people problems. It had just sunk in that this had to change, she had also started to develop serious confidence issues in her surrounding environment, and big ones at that, it made us both miserable; Mia when it was happening and me after it happened, I had to do something, it had to stop.

That same season and another example of when it really hit home was when a good friend of mine became very afraid of going to fetch her own horse, who happened to share the same field as Mia. I was not aware of this for maybe a week or so because we were both at the barn on different time zones, and it was during a weekend that she told me the problem. She said that every time she went to the field Mia chased her out again, and really meant it! I could not believe it, I thought maybe her horse was near Mia and if she wanted to get her horse I imagined maybe she pinned her ears back at her or something like that, but no, what I was about to discover was much more than that. She asked me if I would watch and she would show me, of course I obliged.

Our stables were located at the top of a hill in a small valley situated perfectly so we could look down onto the field the mares were grazing in at that time. I waited there and watched as she walked down the hill, I could hear her open and close the gate as she disappeared behind a hedgerow, and then could see her reappear again as she started to climb the hill now inside the field, that is when it happened. Mia was some five hundred meters away from her and I could clearly see the big and very confident horse lift her head, clock my friend and without hesitation start to steadily canter towards her, not in walk, not in trot, not in gallop, but in canter. On first sighting you could almost believe the horse was running to her, not at her. My friend, and what I think most people would do if they did not know better, simply froze as she saw Mia start towards her and then made what was indeed the biggest mistake you can probably make in a situation like that, which was to run away. She did run, as fast as her legs could carry her all the way back to the gate. Just as she got to the gate, Mia was only a meter or two behind her and had started to pin her ears back in a way that anybody could tell was not friendly, the rest I could not see because of the hedges but could only imagine the worst. I ran down the hill to find my friend on her knees in the mud, she had jumped the gate and thankfully in time. She was extremely upset and at the same time kept telling me she was very sorry. I could not get my head around any of it. We both agreed to go get a hot drink and discuss the situation. In my head I was already diving into a deep wave of emotion.

What am I going to do?
I can't sell her!
Maybe I have to sell her!
She could have killed her!

After a well-deserved cup of tea, I asked my friend why she had said she was sorry and was not angry; after all it was me who should be sorry. She explained it was simply because she understood this meant trouble for me and Mia, and unless we found a solution we would probably have to move barns and that was not what she wanted either. All the while my mind frantically questioned itself.

What if she did this to someone else?
What if she did this to a child?

Thankfully things did work out in the end where I just had to make sure Mia was out of the field when she wanted to fetch her mare, or I would arrange to go with her. Unfortunately and not long after this incident some serious medical issues meant her mare had to be put to sleep. Later on when the heartbreak had lessened, she found a new horse which happened to be gelding, a castrated male, so she did not have to go in the same field as Mia anymore. As far as I know, Mia never chased anybody ever again, or at least it was not brought to my attention that she did, and it is still a bit of a mystery as to how it came about. Understanding horses better today and I hope even more tomorrow, I do have my thoughts on how this could have escalated. I figure that my friend, who is so very kind and sweet, must have been intimidated by Mia at some point and somehow it grew into what I had witnessed. Perhaps the first day she stepped away from Mia a few feet or so and managed to keep the menacing horse away, and after a while this evolved into a few metres and eventually into a chase.

The deep rooted cause of why this horse that socially always appeared quite lazy, and who to this day does not show interest in playing or even grooming with her fellow horse members would go to so much effort, and chase a human being from such a far distance was not clear to any of us at that time, I was at a loss, she really did not like humans at all.

That same year it was a regular life for me and Mia, and besides our issues we had a lot of fun and learned many new things that a three year old horse needed to know. At this point she still never showed me any problems; she was my everything and all I ever thought about day in and day out.

That same summer quite suddenly another situation came to my attention concerning her back legs. They had started to do funny things and quite literally lock in place as if she was paralysed. I noticed one morning after I took her out of the stable, and later that same afternoon when she had been standing on the same spot for a prolonged period. It was very apparent that she had trouble unlocking one of her legs; my instinct told me to ask her to step backwards to unlock it. With great relief it did work, she basically dragged her leg until thankfully it did unlock, but not without leaving ugly superficial wounds on her hooves, coronet band and lower fetlock joint. It did not appear to hurt but let me tell you it is a very scary thing to see, and naturally in the first instance again I called the vet. I explained the situation to them and they, already knowing the horse I was referring to by name because of her previous extended visit for the sepsis, were surprisingly helpful.

It is a very sad story, the more I write and think about our life in the early days the more I realise how tragic it was that she was labelled a dangerous horse and at such a young age. And this was only because sometimes other people had to help her, *yet* she did not perceive it like that. I knew inside it was only going to get worse if I did not find a way to change it.

A vet came to visit, I had been asked in advance to keep her in the stable and restrict her movement until they arrived, thereby exposing the problem. It worked a treat, and the vet who dare not touch her because of previous experience said in so many words:

"It looks like 'locking stifle', but since I cannot get near her for a physical examination the least stressful situation right now would be to give her as much exercise as possible, and sometimes the problem goes away!"

.
That was that, he arrived and left within five minutes. After a day or two I was not satisfied, he had not given me a timeline and even though I was paying him to be there he could not have left quick enough, I can only hope he needed to be somewhere else. I called the vet practice once again explaining to them I was not happy, terrified she would break her neck because it looked awful when it happened, and finally they advised I bring her into the surgery where they could put her in a stock to do a full examination.

A stock is a small area where horses can stand securely with a bar usually made of metal, one on each side, one at the front and one at the back reducing the risk of horses twisting or hurting themselves or the attending personnel. I was actually quite relieved that they did want to help and were thinking of solutions for us in advance. The attending vet must have some credit; he

41

was the first professional at this point in her life who we had not met before, and was someone who tried to befriend her in the first instance. In his experience he instinctively knew that he did indeed have to do something for her, even though she thought it was to, her and before he set about doing anything he worked very hard to gain her trust. I hastily wiped away some tears in a bid not to be noticed as he gave her candies, talked to her, rubbed on her, whatever he could think of really to be able to try and touch her hind legs.

After about forty minutes, although she showed less agitation towards him she would still not allow him to touch her legs. She would show signs of relaxation, even interest in his efforts and within a split second would swish her tail, stamp her feet and if her head was not secured you could pretty much guarantee she would use her teeth mostly because the bars prevented her from kicking. We both agreed that it was in everyone's interest to sedate her so he could successfully examine the limbs and take some x-rays. The injection itself was unpleasant, she knew what was coming after he predictably swabbed the injection site with alcohol, I had to loop the lead rope around the bar that held up the front part of the stock a few times to ensure it was secure enough, so that she could not bite him as he injected her intravenously into the neck. Of course she gave an almighty jump of defiance, I had such pity for her, with all the love I had, I could not help her with this problem.

The x-rays did not reveal much, but after further examination and feeling the joints themselves he diagnosed and confirmed it was the stifle locking. It is a very common problem in horses that are set too upright in the hind limbs. The stifle joint corresponds anatomically to that of the knee joint in a human, and a ligament called the medial patellar ligament. It plays a very important function by hooking over a notch in the end of the femur when the horse is standing still or at rest, to stabilise the stifle, thus allowing the horse to bear weight on the hind joint without using any muscles. It is the very reason horses are able to stand for long periods and even go into a state of sleep. As the horse

moves its leg forwards the ligament will slide out of the notch freeing the leg. In locking stifle the ligament does not slip out as easily because of the angle of the leg and stays in a locked position. Most horses figure out pretty quickly that if they drag their leg for one or two steps they can walk again, they cleverly set the ligament free, she had done just that. Like music to my ears he told me that it does not really hurt and it could be treated non-invasively. It was actually the same prognosis the previous doctor had given me at the barn, but it was great to have a second opinion for such a dramatic and scary problem. He also removed many doubts by saying that because she was so young she may well grow out of it, and in the meantime it would be great if she could be outside more, twenty four hours a day would be ideal. Also that if the problem was still there in four to six months' time, they would revisit the case and look at other treatments. So that is what we did. I received a letter from the veterinary doctor explaining to the barn manager that she needed to be outside for at least twenty four hours that summer. Some of the other horse owners protested, because they felt it was not fair that Mia should get this VIP treatment.
I asked them:

"What am I supposed to do?"

It frustrated me to a certain extent, simply because if it was their horse that had the same or a similar issue they would have done exactly the same thing, the difference being that I would never have questioned it.

The timing of the DVD could not have been more perfect; not only did she need more exercise now because of her locking stifles, what I saw on there made me want to learn more and more, so I could have new ways to ask her to move around from the ground. I will never forget seeing it for the first time. There were lots of different people training and having what looked like a tremendous amount of fun, in a way I had never really seen before.

There were many different breeds of horses working on the ground from a halter and a long rope, or no rope at all, out in big wide open spaces. Wherever their human went the horse just followed. They did things like lay down together, the horses went into trailers by themselves, and there was one man riding his horse with no bridle and no saddle jumping over professionally sized jumps. It was incredible and it looked like magic. The part that really caught my attention was that they could help you solve problems with your horses. You did not need to attend clinics, and you did not need to visit them in the USA if you did not want to, because it was possible to purchase a home training instruction program and watch and learn it in the comfort of your own home. I had never seen or heard of anything like this before and I was sold at the idea. This could be the one way I could help my girl and I was quite adamant about it. I knew it was the only way I wanted to move forwards.

When the study material arrived I studied it all as though my life depended on it. I remember making the executive decision that I was going to watch, read and listen to it all first before I tried any of it with Mia. Then, during the coming period whilst working with her I would watch and listen to it all over again. It took about a week to watch the entire DVD content during the evenings, and in any spare time I had. I made many notes and mentally prepared myself before practicing the necessary exercises, psychology and language to create our new partnership, so that we could head down the path of resolving some of her people problems.

One final event which contributed to her downward spiral of not trusting humans happened not so long after she was diagnosed with the locking stifle. I noticed she was not moving the way she should. I figured it must be down to the same problem, and luckily for us that same day the vet who treated her the last time was already at the barn to visit another horse. I asked if he could take a look. No words would be great enough to describe my surprise when he arrived, because in the past whenever a vet approached, whether they were specifically there to treat her or not, she always protested with her ears back, telling them:

"Don't you come near me!"

Apparently this was not to be her first response on that specific day, and the vet was as surprised as I was when he could reach for her neck to traditionally say hello with a soft pat.

Dumbfounded, I thought: *Was it really that simple?*
It could not be, surely?

Could the cowboy's exercises, which had landed on my doormat a few weeks before, really have started to work so soon? Or was it because Mia had finally decided vets were not all that bad after being sedated the last time she saw one; or maybe she accepted him because he had tried to befriend her before. At this stage, I really did not know. He watched her move around and suggested I get a chiropractor to have a look at her. Without an official examination he said he would not bill me, and told me whatever it was that I was doing for the horse, I should keep it up. I was now very excited and could not wait to share the news with my friends at the barn.
Some of them thought I was crazy, and communicated it to me with sentences like:

"Why on earth would you want to waste your time doing stuff like that?"

This irritated me, and to some extent still can today if I let it.

I would like to take this moment to consider *that* stuff. Many people back then, and still today are usually referring to something they have very little knowledge about. If they had indeed heard of or used this way of training I would have asked them for their advice, because I always want to learn as much as possible. It baffles me how someone can have an opinion about something they know nothing about. To make matters worse, there were other things said like:

"You will ruin her!"

*E*ven though they did not realise I was thinking:
Shit man, she is already ruined.
One girl even stopped talking to me all together.

Tradition can have such a strong hold on people's realities that it is almost robotic, and if another person should dare shuffle their cards they are suddenly a trouble maker or an outcast. Even though really they are doing nothing wrong, except perhaps caring for their beloved horse in different way. Different does not mean wrong. Being the strong person I can be sometimes, in the first instance I did my best to ignore them. I had never really been comfortable with traditional training methods anyway. I went home and continued my studies. I really believed it was possible to do this by myself and would do whatever it took to get that dream partnership.

I made an appointment with a recommended local chiropractor and a few days later she arrived to examine Mia, and give her a treatment if needed. I was anxious to know whether whatever it was that caused her to behave differently the previous time towards the vet had indeed really worked, and that accepting other people coming near her or trying to help her without trouble was not a fluke; or was it going to be a bloody nightmare. During the consultation I explained that she was sensitive, had some temperament issues with strangers, and with pride in my voice said I was currently using some targeted training to help her with her problems.
The lady in question whom we must not forget was being paid a nice sum of money to be of our service, was what you could call, not my type. This was simply because from the very first moment when we met and she had stepped out of her car I did not have a good vibe. To me personally, she was the kind of

person who it was quite obvious had a lot of experience with horses, I did not doubt that or I would not have hired her. The problem was that I could not get her to make eye contact and I do not believe she even heard what I had to say. In that moment I regretted telling her Mia's issues and wondered if the outcome would have been the same had I not.

Just like the vet, she had asked to see Mia move out first on the lunge line in circles and where possible some straight lines. Surprisingly again, Mia who even on her best days could act like a maniac whilst lunging was surprisingly cooperative. After giving me instructions such as walk one way, then the other, then some trot, then the other way, her diagnosis was relayed back to me in a slightly disinterested tone. She told me she could see she had some trouble in her hips and pelvis area, but then followed up with an unpleasant remark in a more sarcastic tone:

"I see nothing wrong with that horse's temper."
Well yes, I thought, *we had not really had the time to explain everything yet.*

The real deal-breaker now was whether she could indeed touch Mia, and by this time, already so early into the appointment, in my mind's eye I could see that it was quickly escalating into a horrid situation. I just wanted her to help me fix my horse if possible and then leave. We took Mia back to her stable and of course here it started. As I look back, this was one of my earlier lessons not just from this beautiful horse, but also in life. I could almost hear Mia say, maybe even demand:

"PROTECT ME"

And for the first time in her life I really did. I finally had the courage to stand up for her and say *NO!*
As I led her back into the stable, and before I had a chance to turn her around in the confined space, the woman kind of pushed the not-so-small horse on the butt, as if to hurry her along as she turned.

Now let's not forget that the horse had just been given a preliminary diagnosis of a problem in the hip and pelvis area, was also learning to live and deal with locking stifle, all of which the lady in question had been clearly informed. In addition to the fact that the mare could be protective and sensitive towards strangers, not forgetting to mention that I was turning with the horse on her outside, and so was in the back of the stable in the far left corner as this woman almost knocked her over. I do not know why she did this; it felt like it came from nothing but a mean place deep inside of her, maybe it was to prove some sort of authority over us, I really do not know. Anyhow, before she had managed to take her arm away, the distressed horse scrambled to finish the turn so quickly that she almost fell down in the process. Thank goodness at least I had decided to use a rope halter, it was enough to hold her back the final centimetres from attacking the foolish woman.

I was furious, not many words were spoken, yet the woman certainly knew she had overstepped the mark. As I tried to settle Mia I did manage to say something along the lines of:

"Would you at least have the decency to shut the bloody door!"

Smartly she did and as she reached to close it, Mia jumped at her again. This was one of the few times where if I could, I would have given that horse a high five, yet at the same time I also could not believe it. Doing my best to stand up for my friend, I told the lady to go away and that I would find her outside in a moment. The situation was not pleasant at all and by this time I was shaking with anger. I took off Mia's halter, left her in the stable where she started to eat her hay again as if nothing had happened, and reluctantly went outside to deal with the woman. As I approached she was already very apologetic, I could say nothing at first.

She asked for me to give her another chance and that she did not realise the situation with the horse was so serious. I asked her:

"What part of the sentence that the horse had problems with strangers touching her did you not understand?"

And in similar many words, asked:

"What gives you the right to push a horse around like that anyway, and any horse for that matter?"

She almost had me believe it was because she wanted to help, and me being me, I fell for it. My whole life and even to this day I try to see the best in people; it always has and probably will continue to get me in trouble for the rest of my days. Not a bad weakness to have I guess, but one that gets me hurt often. In this particular scenario like everyone else I trusted her, and we agreed to give it another go but this time with the horse standing outside. So off I went feeling regret already at my decision and collected Mia to bring her outside, I knew in my gut it was not going to work.

The woman did make an effort to make friends this time, offering her hand which Mia passively tried to nip, and as the woman moved in to try and touch her neck, which I might add was way too soon, she shook her head a few times in defiance, stepped back and swished her tail, not once taking her wide eyes off of the woman. Mia was already saying no, and just as I found enough courage to say:

"You know what, I changed my mind, I will pay you for your time and I think it is best you just leave"

The woman stepped to Mia's side and tried to touch her there, it all happened again so fast. Mia swiftly jumped at her hard enough to knock her to the ground; I do not even recall seeing how Mia did it. The biggest and most final mistake she made was to actually get angry and by jumping to her feet she took a big swing at Mia with her foot directly towards her abdomen as if to kick her. Mia was a few centimetres too far away to receive the blow, so the lady fell back again straight on her backside, it

49

was unbelievable. As she tried to scramble to her feet, she rose this time facing only me; I placed Mia behind me in a bid to protect them both from each other. The next moments took immense courage on my behalf to look at this woman square in the eyes who was a good foot taller than me, and to say something as unpleasant as:

"Get the hell away from me and my horse before I report you, GO NOW!"

Fortunately Mia just stood behind me quietly again, as if nothing had happened. Thankfully she did as she was told and she left, a couple of the girls who happened to be mucking out their stables nearby heard the commotion and came round to see what was happening, it was too late. I did not pay her a penny and we never saw the woman on the premises again, and to be honest I never heard of her again either. After a nice cup of tea and a chat with my friends I decided, following their suggestion, to call the veterinary practice and tell them what had happened. I asked if it was possible to bring Mia to their place, have her sedated in the stock and have a chiropractor come and treat her there. It just so happened they did that quite often and they recommended somebody else who could do the chiropractic treatment.
I believe it was the very next day I took Mia there, and once settled in the stock they mildly sedated her and she was treated. She did indeed have some blockades in her hip joint area and her hamstrings were relatively tight, as for the rest of her body she was in tip-top condition. We did not do a follow-up treatment; I was told to just get in touch if I did not see an improvement in ten days, or of course if it got worse. She looked better already in three days and I was elated, it was all worth it in the end, *or was it?*

CHAPTER 2   Part II

Amongst other things   The dawn of everything and nothing

During those first three years of her life there were a few more incidents, like the odd injury sustained in the pasture either by a kick or scratches from the surrounding trees, and at one point she was infected with ring worm, a gift from a new equine herd member. It sounds like a lot, but these are the risks when keeping any horse in a social environment. Besides these common hiccups life was great, and we had a lot of fun together as she grew into a much bigger and very impressive looking mare. Most horses sustain injuries at some point or another, and once it is treated and they are well again it does not take long for things to be forgotten, unfortunately this was not the case with Mia. After a few experiences I figured out her negative behaviour patterns were so much worse when I was not around, and that it really did depend on the attending person's attitude and intention.
I learned intuitively to just tell certain people to stay away, it kind of became normal to just do that. So normal in fact, that I quickly forgot how it could be if she was not that way. The sad truth is that there really was nobody available who could advise me differently, not without hitting her or using mechanics and tie downs to train her first, I refused to let this happen. Some of the more relaxing times were indeed when she was surrounded by people she evidently did not have a problem with, for example my closest friends. They could touch her, lead her around, change her blankets, feed her and do most things. It really was only certain types of people who either wanted or needed to do something for her, with regards to veterinary or health care, or people who simply just had no *feel* for her.
Remnants of this behaviour can still be seen in her today. Although the need to protect herself with fight has almost vanished, unless a veterinarian doctor needs to use a hypodermic

needle or treat her medically. Again that really does depend on the attending person, and I will share some experiences of that further in the book. Today if she is presented with an opportunity she does not understand or does not like, she will just run away and hide. She would rather choose flight than fight and will definitely see them, or it coming even before they, or it knew they were coming.

When talking about the word *feel,* there are many contexts of what it actually is. With regards to horses it must be felt and experienced with everything we do with them, it is better to feel it than to articulate it. However I will try to explain one perspective; let's say I am in a crowd of strange people and for whatever reason they start to push me from both behind and by my sides, and its effect pushes me onto the people in front of me. I would most likely out of instinct push back, I would probably not care if my elbow dug into somebody either especially if their attitude showed they did not care.

Now what if I was in that same scenario but the people standing in front, beside and behind me were people I cared about, and as they were pushed on to me they would probably try not to hurt me. I would probably try to avoid them and also try not push on the people in front or next to me, that is because I feel for them, I care for them, every cell in my body and every thought I have says: I do not want to hurt you. We must feel the horses; we must touch them like we love them with every single contact, during every single interaction.

You see, if there is one thing I have learned these past two decades, it is that anyone can convince themselves that they have feel for their horses, but if there is one ounce of them that does not completely have this feel, the horses know it, they sense it. And not all, but some horses will let you know one way or another that you actually do not. Personally I do not care what colour, sex, breed, age or temperament a horse has or is, I just know I feel for them all and I am certain in return they know this, not all of them care, but they do know. It is so easily forgotten that horses are the ultimate masters of reading not just our body language but ALL body languages, and having such a small and simple brain compared to ours of course they can misjudge a situation. This is what can make them dangerous and unpredictable because they do not analyse, they only do what they think is right. The reverse of that coin, and what I believe can make them so addictive to people like me, is the moments for example when a horse will make a conscious decision to be around and be with you; there is no better feeling in the world and there are also no coincidences. For this a choice was made, they cannot lie, they cannot cry, it reveals only the truth of what they think about you.

Mia cares about herself with such allegiance and sincerity I can only stand back and admire her. She is a survivor with high regards for her self-worth. In the past she would choose to fight and today if she decides not to stay she will just walk away, or in some cases even run depending on the attending person's attitude and energy. Sometimes people get agitated or upset by this, and I am not just talking about Mia I am talking about in general with their own horses too, it is nothing to be ashamed about. Getting offended and having your feelings hurt are really not what a horse cares about, there really is no need and maybe, just maybe it is a sign to learn something from. Sometimes I smile inside when I see messages and images on social media, or on the World Wide Web reminding us of things like *a horse is the window to our soul* or the *horse is our mirror!*

People see these things, they read them even repeat or share them therefore they definitely know them, but my question is *do they/we really practice them?*

It is hard and unfortunately most cannot and do not, or we would see less frustration towards the horses and more towards themselves if they did. Mia is a perfect example of these analogies; if you do not like her, she feels it and will show you, and if you only like her a little, or are in a hurry, she will feel that too and show you. Yet if you take your time and simply respect her as a living being, she is the sweetest most beautiful animal I could ever have the pleasure of sharing my time with.

One person she just seems to gravitate towards, and whilst in his presence you can see her eyes melt and twinkle with softness, is my father. I think mainly it is because he genuinely likes her, yet he wants nothing from her. He would often joke it was the first horse he did not have to pay for. In fairness that was almost correct; it was through this horse I had become completely independent in my life, or rather she just happened to be in it during that time.

For years through most of senior school right through to my late twenties, and sometimes still today I can be quite shy. I always disliked eating in front of strangers and felt very paranoid should I find myself being the centre of attention. I also dreaded being asked a question in front of more than a couple of people. When I found myself in such situations I would just blush with my heart bouncing out of my neck. It was around this time in fact between 1999 and 2003 I was what you could say at my explorative worst, I had a boyfriend here and there and an on and off social life, and like most young ladies was not happy with the way I looked. I am certain this mirrored onto Mia and unfortunately was a base of some of our issues. I needed her, real bad; as a matter of fact I know I needed her more than she ever needed me. She became my confidant, she planted the seeds of who I wanted to be, needed to be, and could become. Sometimes I watered the seeds and sometimes she did. I have called her my professor for some years now, and to this day until death do us part I will remain her most dedicated student and biggest fan.

That same year in 2003 I was very fortunate to visit Italy with a friend, I liked it so much that I decided to go back that summer for five weeks before Mia was old enough to start some real work. By this time she was huge, not just tall but well-rounded and extremely good looking. We did many things together like attending some local shows where you made your horse look its best and dressed in smart attire, you paraded your horse around in front of a judge, she won many prizes. Another benefit of this was to also explain and show her a small piece of the world, and to gain some life experience before letting her rest on the pastures and grow into her new and powerful four year old body whilst I was away.

I was attracted to Italy because of many things; one of them was my being of an age where for the first time in my life I started to feel very independent. It was a time I could quite possibly be whoever I wanted to be, and it boosted my confidence. What really hooked the fish was my feeling very happy amongst the people I had met, it was great times. It was the same period I met the man of my dreams, a Dutch guy temporarily living there called Jort, *pronounced: Your't*.

He was studying the Italian language and luckily for me was a perfect match. It quickly became a long distance relationship and thankfully not just a holiday romance. The rest of that year I visited him in Italy a few more times before he returned to the Netherlands permanently, and also visited me in England. It was quite the coincidence that during that time the budget airlines were offering flights for ridiculously low prices. I remember one time I flew to Italy for about two pounds, and on another occasion to the Netherlands for six pounds. Naturally I got to meet and know his friends too and found myself also missing them when I returned home.

My employment at that time was fantastic, one I was in no hurry to leave had I not decided to move to another country. I had many friends and a pretty comfortable lifestyle, but eventually after spending long enough getting to know him I was open to explore and try something new. My brother and I travelled a lot with our parents when we were kids, deep inside I always knew I would live somewhere else and quite possibly another country. We had also lost someone very young in the family that summer and it kind of triggered me to follow my heart. So that is exactly what I did and in January of 2005, with reluctant but well wishes from my family and friends, I had Mia professionally shipped to the Netherlands, loaded up my car and followed right behind her. Of course I planned and prepared the whole move in advance, we found a beautiful barn not ten minutes from where I was going to live and so forth. The only thing I did not have was a paying job, but like everything else I was determined to find one and within the first three days of moving, I was at least temporarily employed.

Prior to all of this I had indeed started to ride Mia, the traditional way of saying that is *breaking them in* or *broken in,* and funnily enough I did have at least some knowledge in those days, to plan and set a horse up in a non-violent and comfortable way for their first experiences carrying a human. A kinder term used commonly today is *starting a horse*.

It was relatively trouble free having also invited a few of my girlfriends to sit on her too during those first few days, making sure it was not just me. She accepted them of course, they were *our* friends and after six or seven rides she felt so safe and confident I took her for small hack around the forest. It was as if she had done it a thousand times before and I was immensely proud.

For some reason since the start had gone so well and her ground skills had somewhat improved, my type of training had just as quickly reverted back to traditional as it had started in the new way. Now is as good time as any to admit we still had quite a bit of trouble lunging. It was very difficult to get this big horse going and when I did finally manage it, I could not get her out of my space. Then, when I finally could get her out of my space she would charge around mostly in canter on the wrong leading leg, bucking, rearing and looking like she just had a lot of energy.

My knowledge at that time never saw it as bad training aids, and that the reason she did these things was because I simply allowed it to happen and had no way of correcting it, she was doing what she thought was right. It was not until much later that I noticed we mostly lunged only to the left. An interesting subject if you consider we are taught traditionally to do most things on the left like leading, putting the saddle on, the bridle on, mounting etc. She was placing me on the side she felt most comfortable. I just saw it as something that over time would surely get better and sort itself out, boy was I mistaken. The funny thing is that the

56

training I was now disregarding because my ego was too weak to hold onto it, taught you very early in its training program how to troubleshoot and handle these problems by working with the horse equally on both sides. My brain read it, heard it, saw it, but did not absorb it. In a bid not to make too many excuses my whirlwind romance had distracted me somewhat, and with the added peer pressure and I think basically a simple need for normal conversation (especially when Mia was concerned), this resulted in my new education being pushed aside. In a sense I guess we found some sort of peace together and I often wonder how things would have turned out had I not moved to another country, my gut instinct tells me eventually things would have been the same.

My dedication to her and the previous horses in my life has never wavered and although my social life was more than adequate for a city girl in her twenties, coming home in the early hours from a night out only to be at the barn that very same morning never felt like a burden. Nothing could take away my love and addiction for them. I never grew out of them and at my age now, forty years old at the time of writing this book, I know I never will. Horses are a way of life, a way of life is to have horses. It is an unspoken happiness which I can only hope people find in some other way or elsewhere too.

CHAPTER 2   Part III

Big changes   Forethought and fate

So here we were, I was twenty nine and Mia was soon to be five years old. For the first few months things were great, I had a part time job and I let Mia take it easy while she settled into her new home and environment. The place and location that I chose for Mia to live was, and still is very beautiful, and is one of the better places to keep a horse in the area. Property is extremely expensive in the region which results in in many horse facilities not having much land to let horses roam free for twelve, or twenty four hours a day. What I loved about this particular barn were the various options available. You could choose to have a stable where at night in the winter they would go inside, and during the day they would be outside on large sandy paddocks. In the summer they could go on the fields twenty four seven. These herds were same sex and relatively small, I chose this option at first because it was close to what we were used to back home, but later changed when I realised the other option was actually more suitable for the horses. This meant her living with a much larger and mixed sex herd in a giant paddock with ad lib hay and shelter, where they could roam outside twenty four seven in the winter and then also enjoy the freedom of the land in the summer.

A gateway to the local dunes and beach was on the property and at some point over the next year or so I could remove her iron shoes permanently. Since she was living on a variation of sand and hard ground it was an ideal scenario to go as what is known in the equine industry as barefoot. This is another subject I have gained some knowledge about over the years and wonder sometimes what I would do if I was to move back to England where the surfaces are hard and stony. I am certain with regular hoof care and a suitable diet we could continue without them. Today it is a very controversial subject, one I will not go into too deeply here, like my opinion about putting horses in a stable I have nothing against horse shoes either, it just depends what they are used for and why.

Being in a mixed sex herd did not seem to bother her and as ever she was her big bold self, taking a kick or three when confronted by other horses and only protecting herself when she felt cornered or when she felt it appropriate.

At first we had trouble with the hay because they actually fed haylage instead, and in the first instance she did not eat it, either due to the stress of the move or indeed she did not like it. It was very different to what she was used to and she lost some kilos, but after a few weeks settling in they soon went back on. The trouble with feeding ad lib haylage is that of course you cannot control how much they eat, and over the years we have learned to deal with that. It is not ideal but that is a downside when boarding your horses on somebody else's property, we cannot have everything the way we might find ideal and cannot control the rules. This can leave one in helpless situations sometimes, so the best thing to do is to learn to adapt or simply move.

To be honest it does not matter where we board our horses, there will always be something we do not like about it and in comparison to other barns in the area, it was a small price to pay in exchange for all the other beautiful things we could have.

They were exciting and interesting times, learning the culture and different way of life. A few of the local girls gave me the odd comment here and there on what they thought about Mia's unusual patterns and behaviours. Not always necessarily in a mean way, but they did say something. This was nothing different to the past except sometimes things were said in a different language, and I will admit it was times like that which made me very homesick. I had not made any new and solid friends yet, so felt like nobody had my back if I needed them. Nonetheless we powered on, and I finally found myself a full time and permanent job in the next city from the barn and would often stop by on my way to work to see Mia first thing in the morning. One of the luxuries but something which I missed very much in those early days was that I did not have to clean up after her. All of the chores were done for you, so you could just turn up, take care of your horse and leave after. It was quite the culture shock, since back home this kind of service is called full livery and to keep your horse that way permanently was usually very expensive. Although the monthly rent was quite a bit higher than what I had paid at home, without the additional costs of buying hay and bedding it worked out almost the same with the added bonus of a lot of spare time.

It is funny how things work out; my new employment I had so proudly taken on would soon take up that spare time. As a matter of fact it took around sixty hours per week even though I was only paid for forty. My previous job in England was excellent, with flexible hours allowing me to arrive anytime up to 10:00 and leave after I had worked eight and a half hours including lunch. The new job wanted me to start at 08:00 promptly and as time passed I had so much to do it was in my favour to start at 07:30 if I wanted a lunch break. In some alarming ways it was made very clear they were not happy when I left before 18:30, so most days I left around 19:00. I would work around twelve hours per day, and should I decide to leave earlier the next day I seemed to suddenly have a higher workload on the next.

In hindsight it was some form of emotional abuse which they took advantage of, and the sad part is I let it go on for way too long. I was in a vulnerable situation, they knew this and for nearly nine whole months I endured that shit. I would not have minded, but my immigration meant that some of my qualifications were not recognised in The Netherlands like they were in Great Britain, and I was working in what you could call a downgraded position. The pay just happened to be identical to what I was earning ten years prior.

In a nutshell it felt like I was being told to go to hell, to not complain about it but enjoy the trip. My patience was being tested, but it did not seem to matter too much because at that time thankfully all the other things in my life somehow balanced it out. For a while anyway, that was until certain things started to happen. My once happy self had started to become quite withdrawn, my character and humour took another direction and the most heart breaking part of it all is that my relationship with Mia had also started to change, and I will tell you it was not for the better.

During this time I had not visited home for the first six months, determined that I was going to be happy and make it all on my own to show my family and friends I had made a good decision. At that time it was actually a big white lie, momentarily, but still a lie. I remember it was also difficult to purchase a super cheap flight like the year before which was affordable on my minuscule salary, this contributed towards my not returning sooner. I was indeed very excited to go home having never spent so long away before, however as the plane started to descend I became incredibly sad knowing my parents were waiting to collect me. I secretly cried during the whole landing process, through passport check-out where the guy even asked if I was okay right up to the point where I clocked my mum and dad waving. Upon meeting them, I pulled my chin up and had a great few days at home. While I was there, I realised how homesick I had been but as the days passed this actually reversed, and I found myself looking forward to heading back to my new home again to see the loves of my life, Jort and of course Mia.
It was also around that time during that very trip that I discovered a rather large knot in my stomach when I thought about Mia. Things had not been going right for some months already, she had started to walk away from me when I entered her paddock, when I did get close to her I needed to bribe her with a carrot to get her halter on, and to top that all off she had become less trustful towards me. Any quick movements resulted in her flying backwards and in some instances she protested with her ears pinned back and actually towards me. I blissfully ignored the early signs at first, thinking they would somehow magically pass and of course they did not, they only got worse. It

got so bad that towards the last two months of my employment at that laborious place, my palms would sweat when I arrived at the barn. When time allowed I started to have some dressage lessons with a local instructor. A very kind person, one whom today I often refer to other people, should what I have to offer not suit them.

During the summertime it meant I had to fetch her from the fields and not the paddock, if I could catch her! When I did manage to somehow collect her it meant her running around me in circles, or standing on her hind legs protesting in a bid to deter me from taking her away from what she wanted; quite naturally that was safety and happiness being with her herd. I was no longer anything she perceived as safe or comfortable anymore and to make matters much worse I was very tired, moody, always in a bit of a rush. I myself had fast become everything she did not like about people. I still loved her with all my heart, but she knew I had lost some of my feel for her and I was not giving her one hundred percent. I had been given advice to try lunging her before I rode in a bid to tire her out, so by the time I would get on maybe, just maybe she would be better behaved. This did not work and only resulted in my discovery of that little problem we had forgotten about where she had trouble lunging, it began haunting us all over again. She would run around so uncontrollably fast that she would almost always fall over, and on some occasions she actually did.
The funny thing was I had asked for help and advice as much as I could, and some people did try, but once they realised that they too would fail in their efforts, they quickly resorted to giving up or blaming myself or the horse for our issues, this did nothing for my confidence.

Should I try to lunge her to the right, after a few tries she would simply switch back to the left, kicking out at me with her hind hooves in the process as she passed. Over a period of just a few weeks she was naturally getting fitter and the time it took for her to tire out took something around one hour. I am ashamed to admit that I had let it get that far, to the point where I was sick to my stomach at the very thought of being near her. I shook with fear when putting her halter on and unfortunately she knew it. We also started to develop problems with things like putting her saddle on. She got extremely agitated when I did, so much so that she would bite chunks out of the wooden beam she was tied to. To get her bridle on I had to stand on some steps so I could at least reach her head, somehow we managed. During the rare days when I dared to ride her, she would just take off at a fast trot or canter in a bid to get me off her back, and before long she developed a snappy sharp stop that perfectly ejected me from the saddle, via her left shoulder. She was also incredibly spooky and whatever I did, it just seemed to make things worse. Again there was nobody around who could give me good and solid advice on how to resolve these issues. It was a horrible time for both of us, not forgetting to mention my personality and character was beginning to suffer. My one true love, the one thing I cared about more than anything in the world had grown to what I thought at that time was to hate me. I started to break inside.

During this part of the story a horse's brain and the way it functions must not be forgotten. If you take into account everything I have mentioned so far, her decisions to disagree or control a situation only from the left suddenly become very interesting. Why only lunge to the left, why buck me off to the left, way did she always place me on the left? As mentioned earlier, the answer is actually simpler than you might think. If horses have this magnificent ability to adapt, that means they have to be super learners, and in order to remain safe they are constantly on the lookout for what is best for them at any given time. As tradition would have it, it became normal for people to handle and work with their horses from the left. It is still the same today depending on the human's education. For example, you do not have to observe a riding school too long to witness this. You name it, it is mostly done on the left hand side; from leading them, to tying them, from putting on their equipment like a bridle and saddle, to getting on their backs and getting off etc.

Now if you are a survival species, you are going to get used to this pretty quickly and are probably going to feel pretty safe after a while, because that is the routine and it becomes fairly predictable. So when you feel unsafe or are confused, you are going to look for what is comfortable and that is to have your human on the left.

This information right here is what gets humans and their horses into trouble each and every day, and is pretty much what I am teaching today on a daily basis. You will be much safer and have a much smarter and braver horse if you adjust your habits and skills, and get it to the point where the horse accepts the human on both sides. I mean with everything, walking, leading, lunging, saddling, trailer loading, everything.

Mia would drop me on the left because that was her confident side and that is where she knew me best.

As for the riding itself I had also made a huge assumption. That sweet quiet horse that would often appear solemn, satisfied and content had been talking all along, the problem was that I had not heard her yet. Sure she had a few riders on her back before we made the big move and we did a few trail rides here and there, but the training was not finished yet. I made the assumption when I started to ride her again after the break during our move to the Netherlands that we could start right where we left off. This was a big mistake, mostly because it had not been repeated well enough to reach her long term memory yet, and I should have started her training all over again first. I had also become a different person, I had changes due to our life experiences and I assumed she could handle that and maybe take care of me, she did of course, but just not in a way my human mind could acknowledge. I also did not have some form of checklist to fall back on and I certainly did not know I could have one. The quietness in that horse, the way she would go through things or learn something and then become still and quiet after was the biggest lesson of all, I misread it as obedience. I was very wrong, she had indeed processed certain situations but it does not mean she accepted them. To add one final insight, I cannot be one hundred percent sure but I am certain it helped play a huge part in her development, and that was that each and every time that horse learned something. Whether it be to wriggle away from the vet to be examined or vaccinated, or to fight to get away from the chiropractor, or worse still fight for her hierarchy with other horses, there was always food available. She was constantly rewarded with food. Her survival strategies were rewarded richly; this strong willed and powerful horse was given the fuel to become innocently dangerous, I did not have a clue. She also did not have any understanding of how to yield to and not be afraid of pressure.

Fortunately some of my senses did start to come back during month eight of my horrendous time in that employment. I was incredibly tired, had a few days sick and was consistently making terrible mistakes in my work. Mistakes that actually cost the company money and as you can imagine they were not too pleased. It came to the point where we all agreed I should just leave and that it was best if I worked a final month's notice. The first week of that final month I was sick again due to extreme tiredness, loss of weight and not able to concentrate. With all my heart's intent I was raised well enough to know that I should work that final month like it was my first, especially since I needed to find another job afterwards and I did not want a bad reference. The second week was a blur, I remember handing over some of my work and my colleagues had become very distant. On the third week they actually had the cheek to ask me:

"Why have you even bothered to turn up?"

It was shocking for someone that had worked so hard to be treated in such a way. I heard about it and read about it, but to experience it is just something else, I actually felt abused.

Leaving that job turned out to be a huge blessing in disguise, and something else that came of it was that I did not have to work the final week and a half, which allowed me to restore some of my emotional strength. Fortunately they still paid me my final pittance of a salary and I could move on. It gave me time to think about things and search for a new job. I did find one, in another town in the opposite direction to the barn where Mia lived. Actually I received two offers of employment in fact, from two different companies situated directly next door to each other. This had all happened before that week and a half had finished and I was feeling a lot better not having to go to the other place anymore. Still a little tired, but definitely feeling better I started my new chosen position at the beginning of the very next month. Before this time I had never heard of the term *burnout,* and if I had heard of it I had not taken the slightest bit of notice. I think that was because I had never been exposed to it before, I had just experienced my first.

On a brighter note things were definitely starting to look up as far as my career was concerned, I had a better salary, great benefits, lovely colleagues, regular nine to five working hours, and it was also around that same time that Jort and I decided to move in together. To be honest I only lived upstairs from him, we had not spent a night apart taking turns to stay together in each other's place and we concluded it was a waste of good money so I moved in with him downstairs. He had been very aware of my troubles, and since we were not in a position where we could have horses in our back garden he adopted a Rabbit and Guinea pig in order to cheer me up when I was home in the evenings. It certainly helped and I adored them. He had also persuaded me to take a trip with him and a few friends to New Zealand for six weeks over that New Year. As far as Mia was concerned I was in a huge muddle, and had gone as far as to make the decision of quitting our regular dressage lessons. For the most part she became one big pet that I loved with all my heart, but did not get close to very often anymore because she quite simply terrified me and even if I did, she did not want to be near me anyway.

Some points to mention here are since I had changed my employment and stopped with the traditional training it did not take long for Mia's attitude towards me to soften. I could see and feel that, it was not enough for me to not be afraid of her anymore but I could feel it and although at that time I could not put it into words per se, I knew why. I am very sure that my fear came from a place of frustration, and a problem many people encounter when working with animals is that I had convinced myself that whatever I did or tried, it only made things worse. I felt like I was failing her in so many ways it was extremely overwhelming, I could not handle it so I tucked it away somewhere in my head. It was with all of this information, and the way my mind coped during that time, that I had made a not-so-final decision that it would be best to just sell her. When I finally found the courage to tell Jort, as the words physically left my mouth it felt like my heart had been torn in two pieces. I was devastated, and if a stranger had been passing they would have surely assumed somebody I loved had perhaps just died. It was awful. My love, my dream, my oxygen, my best friend, I was convinced she had to go.

For a few days here and there, I bravely let the thoughts I really did not want to confront myself with enter my head, questioning things like:
Who would I sell her to?
How would I arrange to sell her?
What if she did this?
What if she could not handle that?

It was pure agony. Somehow I held it all together and my first few months in the new job went swimmingly well. My employer was incredibly generous and I was allowed to take the vacation for six weeks, of which three weeks I took as paid holiday and the other three weeks unpaid. It was a bit of blow to my bank balance but my beautiful partner and soon to be fiancé did not let me worry about that.
Just like all of my previous trips and vacation times I arranged for some people to keep an eye on Mia, prayed she did not hurt

herself to the point where she needed physical care and headed off on what should have been a trip of a lifetime.

The sudden change in my working situation and my decisions about Mia had caused me to gain a lot of weight. I always sat comfortably around fifty six to fifty eight kilos and my weight had rocketed to sixty eight. I was pretty depressed about that, especially since the gals and guys we were to hang out with were all at least one foot taller than me and were what I thought super slim and beautiful. Believe it or not it was still the last of my worries, the whole six week trip was one big miserable foggy memory. We did some amazing things and I shall never forget some of the trips and the memories we made together. However, there was still that one thing that just kept nagging at my heart strings over and over:

What was I was going to do with that horse of mine?

The good times we had during the trip lasted momentarily and were quickly overshadowed in my mind by the awful memories of Mia waiting for me at home. We actually spent five weeks in New Zealand with a stop in Malaysia for the final week on the way back home, and it was here something that Jort said changed everything. Seeing my heartache of course he wanted to help and we had discussed certain possibilities and scenarios as to what to do with her once we got home. I had almost found some sort of peace, in another not-so-final decision that I would just retire her and find a farm in The Netherlands or one of our neighbouring countries like Germany or England where she could simply live her life and be a wild horse for the rest of her days, either that or she would end up hurting someone or worse still, herself. He had said

"Why don't you try that other training you told me about again just one last time before you let her go?"

I knew of course exactly what he was talking about and like a big alarm in my head, my brain started to ring. I was so excited that I actually could not wait to leave behind the beautiful paradise we were currently experiencing to get home and see if it would work. In the hope not to sound too selfish here, I just did not care about the trip anymore, it was simply because my relationship with her meant so much more. That night I could not sleep, I remember listening to the soft small waves of the ocean crash against the stilt legs of our cabin in one of the most beautiful locations in the world, wondering if this could really work. Although I dare not admit it out loud too soon, something inside me already knew it would.

CHAPTER 3

The path to redemption   Training without violence

Redemption: the action or process of saving
or being saved from bad places, error, sin or evil.

After travelling not much less than twenty four hours, as soon as
we got home I jumped on my scooter and drove straight to the
barn. Previously I had to sell my car because it was British and it
could only stay in the country for one year on English number
plates. I did not have the finances at that time to change them, so
I had to sell my beloved car and buy the bike. I did not mind too
much, it actually helped clear my mind whilst riding it. It also
encouraged me to use my imagination during times like when I
purchased big bags of feed for Mia and needed to get them to the
barn. I soon mastered the art of carrying large items on my 50cc
horsepower, as any Dutch living citizen would, by either
balancing the bag at the front between my short legs or behind
my seat on the back. I arrived at the barn where Mia was grazing
contently with her herd, and with a lump in my throat only
approaching her up to a few meters away, I said out loud to both
her and the universe:

"It's going to be okay, I am going to fix this."

Around thirty minutes passed and sadly I left without so much as
touching her, but set about to do just that.

The following day having caught up on some sleep, doing the
unpacking, settling into home again and preparing to go back to
work I remembered I had packed a box of videos and CDs when
I moved and wondered if I had also packed those precious
educational videos too. Low and behold and much to my delight

I had, it was a great moment and again I was very excited. Over a few days of research and study I discovered they had improved the tuition program and it was available in a new DVD format, with pocket book guides and charts to help you progress, I purchased them immediately. Every evening as soon as I got home I watched at least ten minutes and then anything up to three hours depending on what our plans were. I was hooked, everything made so much sense and it was like someone had given me a map to the biggest treasure and it was impossible not to try and find it. Jort was amazing, having seen a sparkle in my eyes he had not seen for a while and he encouraged me every step of the way.

With no savings and missing three weeks of salary, I had not yet realised that the tools I was going to need to use were equally as important as the knowledge I was about to learn. Temporarily I had been using another type of halter which was designed and recommended by another horseman. It was not the same as the rope halter I had previously used and I did not really value or understand its use. Having lost or misplaced the one I bought a few years ago I somehow managed to hold onto the training stick and as soon as I could afford to I purchased the rest of the equipment too. This basic equipment is not mystical or magical like some people would have you believe. However it is a key tool to the language and consistency that horses need in order to learn in that particular way. I have some photos of those first weeks where I started to apply these training techniques again. The sad part is that because of my previous experience I was actually too shy and worried about what people thought when they saw me practicing. So for a few sessions I would purposely go out of my way and even further out of my comfort zone by taking her up towards the entrance of the dunes situated a few minutes' walk from the main barn area and practice there. One picture depicts beautifully Mia's thoughts towards me and my decisions showing just how tall she could be when she would rear up and say:
"No, I cannot." or *"I do not understand."*

Having been fortunate enough to be around horses since I was quite young, I learned hard and fast that I knew nothing about them, the horse was talking and I had not been listening. I was starting to acknowledge many sad truths and one of them was that she did not want to be with me, she wanted to be with the safety and comfort of her herd. A realistic fact and one I did not resonate with much at that time was that it did not matter how much money I spent and how many kisses and cuddles I gave her, she really did not care.

With all my best efforts, being away from the barn area frightened me so much that after a few attempts I decided to ignore the stares and unwanted comments, and started to work with her in the round lunging pen located smack bang in the middle of the barn. Thankfully my logic and some willpower had kicked in, it was much safer for both of us and if for some reason I had to let her go she could not run very far. This was a turning point, my training and belief had started to become stronger then people's opinions. In my heart of hearts and as hard as it was, I knew I was not about to let these people stop me doing what I believed in again. After all they did not have any answers, not ones that did not have involve some form of violence or taking the horses dignity away anyway. I was so desperate that if somebody offered me advice of course I listened but in the end it was always the same answer, they either did not have one or they blamed me or the horse and still with no real solution.

It was around week three, I can remember distinctly that although she was still showing me some resistance and although I was indeed still afraid, my fear started to manifest from another place inside. I am sure it was because I found a new place of certainty and because I had answers for some of her questions. Something had started to change and her negative responses towards me became shorter. It really did not take very long, and in my journals I made a record during that week that she was unusually quiet, I was concerned she may be ill and soon discovered she was not, she was just extremely relaxed in my company and I had simply forgotten how that looked. I was also starting to realise that like all the times before that, when Mia was quiet she was actually learning something, she was processing. The difference was that during these times it was actually in a positive way. In such a short time we had made huge changes together. An important detail and one that I try to encourage people to do as much as possible, is to go out of their way to at least understand why things are done in a certain way, not just how, especially before they make any form of judgment. I mention this here because it made our progress much harder than it needed to be, and personally I am not the kind of person who can simply ignore stuff like that. Although at times I admit I can be incredibly naïve, I am not stupid and I am very sensitive to people's feelings and emotions. Until not so long ago this was something I used to feel was a burden, but now I have learned to see it as a gift. And because of this it does not take long for me to find out if somebody does not like me or is talking about me or my horses and this really is OK, it is just life. I can usually figure it out because of an uncomfortable or reluctant conversation with said parties' friend, partner or sibling and the way their body language reacts.

An example of some more bullying we experienced is of one day whilst blissfully going about our business, I walked with Mia contentedly after a successful session together with a spring in my step and felt extremely happy. Someone who had been watching in the background stepped out in the narrow path in front of us and physically blocked our way through. Pushing my shoulder back in a singular and unfriendly motion they said:

"You should not be doing what you are doing, it is bad for the horse and you need to stop!"

Astonished at this remark I took a deep breath and asked Mia politely to step backwards out of our now-invaded space, and with as much tact as possible I responded:

"I had no idea you knew what I was doing, can you tell me how long you have tried this way of training?
Because of course I would love your feedback, and to hear the things that went wrong for you, maybe I can learn from them?"

Looking at me somewhat puzzled, they now stepped back out of our space and said in a lower more careful tone:

"Well, I cannot tell you because I have not tried it. But I will tell you I will never do it, because I do not like what I see".

Trying not to sound irritated I responded:

"So you have gone out of your way to give me an opinion which I did not ask for, only to explain to me that you do not like something which you know absolutely nothing about?"

As they stuttered to say: *"No, what I mean is!"*
I was finished with the conversation, and using my body language I indicated that we were done and continued to walk by. They stepped aside and rightly so, the presence and size of the big beautiful horse walking behind me was enough to move four people. I can tell you I am not alone when I say I have had to have this type of conversation hundreds of times since, and probably will for the rest of my life, it has become second nature.

It is only humans' nature to undermine something they do not understand or believe in, I just think as a species we need to learn to go about these things another way and figure out a way to offer solutions instead of constantly presenting problems. The beauty of all of this was that in the training program they had started to teach me about humans' emotions, both mine and other peoples. I was not only learning how to handle the emotions of the equine species, but also how to handle the human species themselves and in some cases at an extreme level. These confronting situations which in the past I would have let destroy me, were now becoming tools to grow. I had begun to master the

74

art of answering them with their own question. Therefore in return my confidence grew, not just with Mia but also with real life situations. My brain was learning that it did not matter what people thought or said, it only mattered what she thought and said. When finally I could see that she was in fact looking for answers and searching for ways to meet me in the middle, I made a complete one hundred and eighty degree turn in my psyche and gave her something I had not done for a long time, I gave her my heart and mind one hundred percent quite simply because I found the keys to believe in us again.

So the beginning of 2007 was very impressionable, most certainly life changing, and I have never looked back. My visits home to England became more frequent, and having grown roots in my new home I felt like a tourist when I returned to the UK. A life changing moment I will also never forget was one day while taking Mia for a walk in the dunes together, Jort got down on one knee and asked me to be his wife. I was ecstatic, it was like a fairy tale, it was scary too. I had committed to permanently living in the Netherlands with my devoted fiancé and away from my family and friends. This new future naturally made me feel uncertain, yet at that same time it also felt very right.

The best memories of those early days were returning to some of my old habits again, and that meant going to the barn again before work to visit and sometimes work with Mia. It was enchanting to be there so early on such a beautiful location, surrounded by the birds singing in the trees and the added bonus of nobody around to poke their nose in my business. I could simply choose which facilities we needed to use that day, which in return allowed us both to progress at lightning speed. The things that used to terrify me dissipated into beautiful yet simple habits and skills. It was the simple things, like putting her halter on, which simply became nothing short of an understanding partnership. Rather than make her put it on, instead I could teach her how to help me put it on. Rather than just walk somewhere by dragging her, or lets be completely honest here, her dragging me, we learned how to walk together on both her left and right side. If there was some form of resistance, I learned how to drive her forwards instead of pulling her forwards, and at the same time respecting and helping her with thresholds.

This is a small example, as there was and is so much more. Something that was equally significant was that I had learned how to communicate in a way she could understand. What was once our most dreaded subject fast became one of our better skills! Our lunging had evolved from a wild and uncontrollable mess, to beautifully choreographed circles both with a line attached and at liberty where there is no line attached. I had learned to match her energy and not her emotions, therefore giving her time to connect and ask questions. In fact so many things were going on, I did not realise how many seeds I had planted until much later. Encouraged to keep a journal of our progress, I did just that, it can help remind you how far you have come and aid with motivation when times are challenging.

Sure it was not perfect, I had absolutely no help from a professional until later in 2008, so I was indeed self-taught, but I can tell you with every cell in my body I was so delighted having found a way to train my horse and in a way I liked, it just made so much sense. All that mattered in the end was that I could indeed keep my Mia, all the thoughts and ideas that she would have to go to some other place had disappeared. The ingredients to the icing on our cake were that we had started to like each other again. Of course I asked myself that niggling question: *Why did I not continue with this back then?*

The truthful answer I can come up with is:
Because I was not ready then and this time I was!

Here we were, now able to do many things together, things I had only dared to dream of. We had started to do some of the things I saw on that first video which had landed on my doormat some years before. If you had asked me a few months prior, I would have never thought it was all possible. Yet there was one thing still tugging at my heart strings on occasion, and this was because I had not dared sit on her back again; this came about a little while later and I will come back to that shortly. As we progressed, our presence started to cause an unusual stir in some of the people at the barn. Considering that on most days I would go in the morning to avoid them, on the days when I did go during the daytime, on the weekends for example, we started to get interesting and more welcoming remarks like:

"Which horse is that?" or *"Did you buy a new horse?"*

The amusing part is that some of these comments came from the very same people who gave me unwelcome opinions only months before. And although they did not have the answers to help us, they were dead certain that these ancient training techniques were not going to work, even though they knew less about them than I did. I am not mad at them or the situations we all found ourselves in, if I am honest I am only thankful to these people, and I will say it over and over because they helped make me grow stronger when I needed it the most. Of course back then, and when it happens today it hurts, and sometimes I can let their emotions influence mine to the point where I can feel like crap. But that is not what is important here, the message I want to get across is that if you truly believe in something, you have got to give it a try and if possible give it all you have got. If you quit because somebody told you to, what kind of life will you have and how will you ever get things done?
It is a gamble yes, but *isn't everything in life?*

Things take hard work, indefinite hours, dedication and perspiration, especially if you are troubleshooting like I was, and any kind of work where live animals are concerned can be dangerous, period. I used both the negative and positive remarks of others to give us ammunition, one of the results of which just happened to be that a small handful of them genuinely did not recognise Mia as the same horse anymore. Some people were adamant that I had exchanged my horse and others were intrigued and very happy for us both. At last we had started to feel comfortable in our skin. Unfortunately that was until some further events happened at the barn where I felt completely helpless. In the end it compelled me to make the decision of moving her away to a new home.

The first incident happened one day when I arrived at the barn and found that she was crippled in pain, she could not place her left front hoof on the ground, it was very scary and she was obviously in a lot of pain. It was confirmed by a vet after a short visit that she had an abscess inside her hoof, due either to the fact that I had taken her iron horseshoes off, (this can happen sometimes when the hoof changes shape too quickly), or to something such as the diet being changed too quickly from haylage to grass.

Although very nasty, I was to find out it was very common in the Netherlands and with certain traditional treatments it was curable and could be completely over inside a week. I am happy to report it was, however she needed to rest in a stable for a few days because she was vulnerable and could not walk. I was provided a stable temporarily where she could rest and recover, but since all of her friends were outside on the fields she could not relax and drove herself crazy. I was prescribed some oral medication to lightly sedate her to help her rest; I was reluctant at first but will admit it did help take a slight edge off her agitation. She did quieten down but would still look over the door at every opportunity to call out to her friends and let them know where she was.

I had a sleepless night worrying about all the worst possible scenarios and unfortunately my fears were confirmed. I arrived the next morning to find her nose extremely swollen, so much so that her face was not recognisable as a horse anymore. It appeared that she had somehow hit her nose so hard on the bar on top of the door that it would have been a surprise if it was not broken. Another call out from the vet confirmed it could well have been broken, but he reassured me at this stage that as long as she was breathing normally, was not coughing or struggling for air, could eat and drink, and of course if it did not get worse, then she would be fine and we would be able to know and see more once the swelling had subsided.

After a few days of medication and treatment her hoof abscess cleared up and her nose did indeed get smaller, and to both our relief she could return to the pasture again. She allowed me to gently touch her nose and eventually showed little if any evidence of pain, and considering our relationship the last two years she was very patient with me. But you could tell for a while emotionally that there had been a trauma by her shying her head away in response to quick movements, especially human arms. A few more days passed and whilst collecting her from the field, I had trouble asking her to help me put the halter on; she wanted to but just could not. We had built so much more trust by that time that I could actually just walk her back to the barn with the rope around her neck, however a witty remark from one of the other horse owners quickly discouraged my confidence and convinced me that I needed to put the halter on because it was dangerous.

To keep the peace I agreed, in retrospect she was to some extent right, there were after all children around, so with a little struggle I did just that and put her halter on. I led her quietly to the area designated for you to groom and clean your horse and secured her with a traditional knot to the wooden hitching post. I already knew my mistake as I did it and within what was only a split second or two she pulled back. She pulled back so hard and fast that she started to panic and as she panicked the pressure of the halter pressed down on her nose in the area which was now violently painful. Trying to avoid getting hurt I attempted to release the lead rope and then it happened: a yellow and green substance started to shoot out of her nose, like tubed toothpaste, it was no picture for the faint hearted and quite unbelievable. Subsequently it covered nearly most of the wooden beam, the floor area around her front hooves, her front legs, my entire arms, hair, face and mouth. One could compare it to squeezing a huge zit with the added and very unpleasant bonus of ultimately smelling revolting.

It was one of those life moments that while it was happening seemed to go in slow motion, you were very aware of what was happening yet were somewhat useless in your own response and then before you know it's over.

Within seconds she had stopped panicking and it was as if the infection that had been laying quite dormant and hidden away inside her nose was now gone and she just stood there with her head low licking her lips looking somewhat trivial but relieved. I was in what you could fairly call a state of shock and some of the other horse owners who happened to be around were too. Once again without hesitation I had another reason to call a vet. They confirmed indeed it was an infection from the accident and that perhaps there was small piece of broken bone causing the trouble. The infection never came back and from that day forth I do not remember any more trauma come from it, except that one day while grooming her face, as I ran my hand down the long bone which forms the nose I could feel a tiny dent. So there it is ironically I could have named this story:
The horse that broke two legs and its nose!

With that said, the situation might have been made much easier for my dear sweet Mia, had she been allowed to have a companion when she was confined to the stable for rest, but the rules of the barn at that time did not allow this and I could not help but feel a little bitter about that. I can with some satisfaction confirm today that it was because of this situation the rules started to change.

The second incident was not long after, and unfortunately went back to that same old subject of strange people with no feel dealing with Mia, and who went against my wishes. Before I continue, I will add that although it was an unpleasant and very unwelcome situation, everybody involved learned a great deal from it. Today I have no bad will towards any of these individuals, but chose to share this story because of its educational value. Because of her issues I had made a deal with the barn management that I would do things such as orally de-worming her myself, purely because it was better for everyone, and we had grown accustomed to doing this for many years already. De-worming a horse this way is usually performed every six, eight or ten weeks depending on a set worming schedule, and I thought I had explained very carefully our special situation. For reasons I cannot begin to understand, a small handful of people who thought they were helping had decided I had not been clear enough, and naturally having being around horses for many years they took matters into their own hands, and went against my wishes. I so dislike decisions like this made by people who with all intentions might mean well, but in the end do not think these situations through enough. This is another time where all my fears were confirmed again by Mia being in a helpless situation and feeling like she really had to protect herself, so much so that she almost killed somebody, two people in fact.

Somehow they managed to get her halter on, and I heard later a juicy carrot had been on offer so she had half willingly let them. It did not take them long to discover that whilst out in the open space waving around the oral syringe, which in her mind probably looked not much different to a hypodermic needle and syringe, was most definitely not going to work. They decided to put her in a stable where they figured she could not run around as much, and thought they could have some sort of control over her. What a big mistake, with that action undertaken they now had a horse that was not only very frightened and trapped, it also had feeling and the need to protect itself. It was here they made another stupendous decision: by running a long rope from her halter between her front legs, then around her rib cage, back though her front legs and back through the halter. A very old fashioned technique apparently used in order to teach horses a lesson and show them that humans are the boss. The idea was that by pulling on the rope they could take control of her head and neck by using her own body strength and at the same time cause her to submit.

I can only take my hat off to them for succeeding on getting the rope on her like that, but if I ever heard such a story again my destination would most certainly be behind bars. Ironically, I had arrived at the barn a short while after the said event, where she had no choice but to nearly kill these people. It was such a commotion, I was instantly surrounded by many good doers who had all been there to witness it, and who could also not wait to tell me what had happened. This was before I even had the chance to remove my helmet, let alone get off of my scooter. I could not hear or figure out what had happened in the irrational environment, it was so chaotic that for a moment there I thought Mia was seriously hurt or worse, dead. My heart and brain could not absorb what I was hearing until somebody finally took me aside to explain. It turns out that my horse, who nobody had been given permission to touch like that in my absence, had almost crushed one person by severely bruising their ribs, and amazingly had not killed the other one, because she had felt the need to rear up and come down on them. Luckily, they only escaped with a few scrapes and bruises.

Worse still, I was put in a situation where I was supposed to feel bad for them and they expected an apology. I was furious. That was a boiling point for me and my emotions sped out of control. The person who took the time to explain the situation to me at least mentioned that Mia was fine and back in the pasture with her buddies. With that knowledge, I immediately went on a search for the hurt individuals. They were still standing around seeking comfort from bystanders because of my naughty horse. They saw me approach and I tell you it was not a pretty picture, I had to be held off of one of them and the other one just started to cry. I was done with it all, and after realising that whatever I said was not going to be heard, as soon as I got home I explained the situation to Jort and set about searching for a new place for her to live.

I found one, not too far from the location of my employment which in some ways was quite a luxury, and should I want to I could visit her in my lunch break too. It was one of the very few barns again which had land and the horses could have some sort of life living outside. A bit of a factory really with some two hundred and fifty horses living on its premises, they also catered for competitions so it was always extremely busy. I was super excited at the prospect of the facilities on offer though, with three indoor arenas, two outdoor arenas, three lunging pens of which one was covered, a park to explore just next door and the best part was her housing which was made up of two parts, where the horse could live half inside a stable and half outside in a small private terrace. I never saw a stable like that before and for the next two years we had some life changing and fun times; it was here my horsemanship journey really took off. I stuck to my regular schedule of going to the barn before work to train her, and found much satisfaction again in taking care of her needs with things like mucking out her stable, only to return again after work and give her what she needed until the next day. Only equestrian lovers can understand the therapeutic value behind these simple gestures, and the gratification of knowing that everything is the way you like it. I became engrossed in my training and working on becoming a better person, knowing that one path on that road less travelled would eventually lead to her trusting other human beings.

There were certain areas of the barn that we had a fair amount of trouble with, like walking past the big cow shed. She was not having any of that and with no self-confidence for those type of things, appeared quite literally terrified. Going into the arenas especially when going from light to dark was also quite a daunting experience, but by sticking to the principles and using what I had learned I soon won her confidence.

I remember walking around the barn with her during those first few days still holding onto some older habits, and one of them was to clasp the rope directly under her jaw to walk her around. It is really quite absurd for us to think that we have better control of a horse by doing this, at that time she weighed something close to six hundred and fifty kilos and myself a mere sixty five.

She had shown me numerous times in the past that without much effort she could quite literally lift me off the ground with just her head. I knew that what I was doing was not helping us, and from what I had been learning I did have a new picture in my mind of how it would be. The way I see it and the way I have been taught is that if you have the vison of how you want to see something first, it will help you with the end result. My new picture was holding the rope at least halfway along its length so the belly of the rope touched the ground, walking together at the same pace contentedly. Some might think this was a small achievement but to us it was huge, simply because I wanted to be able to do this everywhere and not just in certain places. The knowledge of how to do that and at the same time be able to walk past the cow shed or into the arenas with a loose rope and relaxed horse mostly meant that you had to understand horses first, and know why they have these reactions in the first place. Horse psychology is becoming hard and fast a normal thing today, the information I was learning back then was not available like it is today and that is my answer for somebody reading these particulars thinking:

"What was the big deal?"

Without going into too much detail as to how I actually trained her and helped her overcome our fears, I will share examples of how it got better in the hopeful prospect that those who have similar issues may well be triggered to search for answers too, because they are all there, you just have to look hard enough and be brave enough to take the first step. This book is not designed to teach you the horse training program itself, and I will tell everybody it is a way to train and be successful with horses both on the ground and riding in any discipline. Just like any training program the technique, skills and methods are not magic, you have to make it work and you have to stick to your principles, you also have to have a suitable attitude.

The first day I was brave enough to allow my picture to become a reality will stick in my mind forever; it was a proud and lucid moment. I can tell you with the utmost conviction, had my confidence in what I was doing not been where it was, I am not sure of my alternate response in the next scenario. I found myself responding rather appropriately even though my confidence in people was still relatively low. I will not lie and say it did not feel uncomfortable, it really did and it certainly stirred up some of the horrible feelings of hurt and pain caused by the past, but it was a start. Whilst walking around at the very back of the huge premises where the trailers were stored on a large car park, a lady who had been inadvertently watching came running up to us and said:

"What you are doing is dangerous and did you not know that your rope is dragging on the ground?"

I smiled at her warmly, and without trying to sound sarcastic I responded:

"Oh, so it is."

And without changing a thing proceeded to walk. I felt like the better part of me had come to life and this was huge in my personal development. She did not know why we walked together like that, evidently it was wrong for me to allow my horse the choice to walk next to me rather than me holding her next to me. The point is that standing up for both me and Mia was becoming a normal thing and I found myself getting less upset about it.
It felt amazing.

CHAPTER 4   Part I

Calm before the storm   Sometimes believing is all you have left

> ***Friend:*** A bond of mutual affection,
> companion, soul mates.

I read a quote once by somebody called Blaise Pascal which said:

Humanity's problems stem from man's inability to sit quietly in a room alone.

If we were to count how many hours your average horse owner spends with their horse per week including the everyday chores like general care, grooming and riding, it would probably amount to much more than one would care to admit. And if we were to count how many of those hours were spent actually hanging out with the horses doing nothing, then that too is usually a lot less than one would care to admit. Tradition, culture, environment, time and lifestyle can all have an influence on how we keep our horses, and if you consider that horses are social animals and love to hang out with each other including us, you would think it was logical to actually do so, no matter where you live on this beautiful planet.

Ironically this is not always the case, and one of the exercises I had learned and quickly grew to love was to actually spend time with Mia doing nothing, just like horses do with each other. This type of exercise is best executed in a relaxing place and ideally where it is just the human and their horse, for Mia and me our new stable was a perfect place.

One of the rules is to try and not touch the horse unless it is absolutely necessary, for example to protect your personal space if they show curiosity with their nose, mouth or explorative hooves. We had become quite busy with this almost every day for the first few months and sometimes when work was less busy I would take an extended lunch break just to go and sit with her. It did not take long for me to see that the end result was simply remarkable. It was here Mia had begun to give me one of her personal teachings of how to seal the deal permanently on our friendship. This reminded me fondly of the memories during that first week we spent together when she was still untamed. Ironically, I realised that the extra time we had taken to get to know each other then, had been a similar ritual.

To ultimately test our relationship I made sure there was hay and water available and as the initial days passed she would stand and eat for ten, maybe twenty minutes before she decided to show any real interest in me. As the consistency of the exercise was established and after making myself comfortable usually in a corner sitting on an empty upside down water bucket, she would start to turn her attentions immediately towards me. It started with her coming over and nudging me with her nose to softly and inquisitively investigate my hands. Sometimes she would lift a front leg to touch me with a hoof as predicted by the instructions, so quietly but passively I used my arms from side to side or up and down by gently slapping my lap to discourage the unwanted behaviour. Every single time there was a new and breath-taking discovery, I was hypnotised by her curiosity, softness and willingness and the considerate decision she would make about how to stand directly in my presence. These moments used to make my jaw ache in a bid to hold back tears, this big beautiful horse that not so long ago terrified me was now opening herself up using her own language, one that even after all of those previous years with horses I was only just beginning to sincerely understand.

There are three favourite positions that she has, one of them is standing with her body and head positioned so her two eyes and long nose are square in front of me. Then millimetre by millimetre her head will fall into my lap ending with a drool patch and droopy bottom lip resting on my knees. Another is to gently park me by her side at her underbelly and every minute or so she will edge closer and closer until I am practically underneath her. Still today my personal favourite is when she will stand close by, and usually over just a few minutes she will inch herself closer and closer so I end up under her neck and between her front legs as if to protect me, not much different to a mother and her foal, and then sometimes in her snooze she will cock her head and look down directly as if to check that I am still there. I would spend anything from ten minutes to two hours sitting with her, sometimes taking a book to read while she stood there with what I can only assume was contentment and happiness.

A month or so into this practice, she had chosen the standing directly in front of me position where she would eventually end up with her nose on my lap, except this time she was curiously busy with a new idea of not leaving my hands alone. Horse's noses are incredibly versatile and resourceful. It is quite a remarkable piece of anatomy, acting not much different to our hands. With such softness and care she repeatedly used her lips to turn over or open one of my hands and gestured for me to lift it up. At first I misread her questions and I would instantly drop my hand on my lap, she would then insist on playing with my hands again until one of them was up in the air and after a few of her patient attempts I realised what she was asking. I cannot express enough the emotions of what I felt and as it registered, she was not asking me to touch her actual face, she was asking me to touch her aura. I found this out quickly too because if I did touch her face or accidently brush an eyelash or whisker she would move her head away telling me that was not the answer either before starting over again.

If I clearly stroked the atmosphere around her face she immediately became solemn and quiet, it was so very obvious because her eyes, ears, energy and very being told me just to embrace her request. It was also her famous quietness that told me she was processing. In not so many words I truly believe that by giving her what she needed, she gave me what I needed and in return we were rewarded with what we both really needed, and had been searching for, which equated to nothing more than an authentic and mutual way of really being together.

Being an extremely sensitive person, although not as much as in the past, I can easily wear my heart on my sleeve and am very open to things like people, their thoughts and feelings, the planet and general life. That said, I never had much of an interest in natural healing or things like energy work, evidently Mia did. I learned that she was showing me some form of healing touch or a form of reiki, and the more I think about it I cannot help but be captivated and enchanted by her suggestions. If we are to talk about healing without a particular reference to a higher power, Spiritualism or the cosmic universe, but just between one individual and another, then I will agree wholeheartedly that somehow she showed a way to heal us and I can only hope in return somehow I did the same for her. Talk about good timing, it was a perfect moment in our life and it felt like she was telling me in her own way:

"Keep doing what you are doing, I like it!"

Today is no different except that our mutual understanding of these moments together has matured. There are no words to describe the feeling each and every time, and I will often sob as she reminds me just how special she is and how far we have come. Sometimes by laying down next to me, and other times having complete comfort knowing that if I kneel down in front of her and gently rub my hands together, she knows that as soon as I open them she can place her head between them so I can caress her aura. It is in these moments I can forget everything in the world, its troubles and sometimes mine.

One sunny morning whilst working with her in one of the indoor arenas, the birds were singing in the rafters and the bright sun glared through the huge glass windows that dominated the long side of the building. It was very warm and as I stopped to wipe the sweat and dust from my face two girls appeared standing in the doorway watching and obviously talking about us. I shuddered at the thought that perhaps they would interrupt me and give me unwanted advice, but to my surprise they left only to return the next day. With big smiles they caught my attention and told me that they too were using the same training and that they had to be somewhere else the day before, so decided to catch me again another day. It was so nice to finally meet people who were doing what we were doing and with whom I could actually talk about it too, I was super excited.

Just a few days before, somebody had left a postcard on Mia's stable door and the front picture displayed a witch on a broom stick. Whoever left the card wrote:

"Dear Zowie, please stop with your hocus pocus!"

In the past I would probably have burst into tears and been very hurt over such a situation, not this time. Instead I took the card straight to the big notice board which hung in the public canteen area and wrote a message back clearly under theirs in black marker:

"Dear friend, please watch out, I also practice BLACK MAGIC, greetings ZOE."

One could argue it was a childish act to play their game back, but I will not deny I had some satisfaction out of it. Having been told especially lately what people thought about me whether I liked it or not, my little devil was awoken and now I could actually laugh about it. I also discovered later that a bunch of adults who often hung out together to drink beer more than they actually did anything with their horses may well have been the culprits. In passing one day with Mia by myside they shouted out some ludicrous sentence in Dutch with *hocus pocus* mangled somewhere into it. I just smiled, sarcastically clapped my hands towards them and went about my business. Later that same day I found that someone had keyed my car all the way along the driver's side. A coincidence perhaps, but if you consider the space next to me was the end of the car park with plenty of room for even a tractor to get by, I have my doubts. Later that same week, I found Mia's beautiful mane had been cut in an ugly way with scissors too, I kid you not. If I was a mean person, maybe I would have deserved some of this treatment but I was not, I was just perhaps a bit odd because of my preferred way of training. The shame of it all I guess only hangs on their heads.

Thankfully this was soon forgotten, I had scheduled to go on a very exciting trip with Mia and we were finally heading to our first training camp with real Professionals, who were qualified to teach what I had been learning. Although I had heard great things about him, I had not yet met the only instructor officially teaching this way, located at that time down South in the Netherlands. He just happened to be teaching a five day camp together with another instructor from Switzerland less than one and a half hours drive away. I was overjoyed at this opportunity and nothing could stop us attending, it was a new beginning on our educational journey. Having been self-taught, I had to make some changes and adjustments to things which cannot necessarily be taught in a video. It was difficult at first and way more challenging than I had ever imagined, but once I had the feel for how to do it, we were quickly on our way. I had to learn to accept that some things we had practiced, I had simply not done enough of yet and other things I had not done at all, mostly because my brain was not ready for the information yet. However I was pleasantly surprised to find we were indeed doing just fine.

With the utmost enthusiasm and doing my best to understand the *why* and not just the *how,* I did as I was told and it paid off immensely, just three days into the course I was learning how to ride one day without a bridle in big open areas. The instructor soon became a regular mentor and as the years passed became a good friend too; it was because of him Mia was able to recover after her near fatal accident.

It was during that first clinic that I had taken the first steps to riding her outside again, it was not easy and I will not pretend that after a few times riding on her back in the safety of an arena that I was magically cured, it actually took another year before I felt completely comfortable. Even under the eye of an instructor it took a lot of courage for me to ride out in the open with other horses around. The only way to overcome a fear like that is to start tackling the problem from its stem and then piece by piece learn how to re-train the brain and survival instinct to search for other answers to replace the apprehension. It worked, and naturally everything else I was learning became better than it had ever been before, not just with Mia but with all of my previous horses too. We had accomplished so much, the things that used to scare us had vanished, the uncontrollable behaviours that used to terrify me were gone and the horse that not everybody could touch was now more *touchable*.

The vaccinations were still a problem, fortunately for us there was a veterinary practice located on the actual premises and after my familiar and usual explaining of her issues, the doctor quickly recognised our troubles and agreed that indeed it was better for everyone if I did the injection myself. In hindsight because everything else was going so well and since I only had to give the injection once a year it did not feel like such a big problem anymore. However the issue was still there and would soon catch up with us again.

That same year Jort and I received the keys to our first official home and that summer I had one of the best days of my life by marrying him where we met in Italy. This man who having only known me for a few years prior saw the good in me and never doubted my ambition and try. Apart from my parents he was one of the first people I can remember that accepted me for who I really am, I know I am lucky.

In the spring of 2009 having resided on that particular farm for almost two years and having attending regular clinics, we had grown and adapted our relationship to a place you would have never recognised a few years before. Finally we also had enough funds to replace my now exhausted scooter with a small car, it was a nice luxury to have one again. One afternoon I decided to drive and visit the barn where I had boarded Mia previously to see some old friends. As I walked around I found myself admitting:

"Shit I miss this beautiful place."

The location where Mia had been living since, although it was sufficient, lacked something that I missed terribly and that was the gift of nature. The whole location was like one big concrete horse city, no trees in between the stables, buildings and roads and if you did want to see a bird fly in the sky or witness a blade of green grass, then you had to go to the back of the property where the horses could go outside or take a walk down the long path that took you into the neighbouring park instead. I remember noticing this the most after returning from that first training camp which had been held in one of the prettiest nature parks in Holland, and as we led the horse back to their stables I saw immediately how grey and dull the place looked. The horses did not care as long as they had their food, but still it felt somehow significant. Because of this the atmosphere and energy of the place fast became depressive and the more visits we made away from there where we were surrounded by trees and nature, the more I disliked it.

As I walked by the outside arena I saw six, maybe eight girls working with their horses in a way of course I now recognised. I could not believe it, one of the girls who had been a working student of the instructor down south now kept her horse there too and was giving a training day. It was a big wake up call and a pleasant surprise, I was sold. I had to give one month's notice to both locations and with great joy could move her back. Of course I made it very clear under no circumstances was anybody to give Mia things like a de-wormer paste or vet treatment without my permission, the event that had happened before had not been forgotten, it was not a bad thing really because it helped seal that deal in gold. I am certain they never really had a space for us since I was not allocated storage for my equipment until a month or two later, but I did not care and was so happy to be back there. Mia was reunited with her old friends and I found the extra time not having to take care of her stable and needs very useful again by putting it into our training. A lot of the same people were still around and many new faces too, it was an amicable feeling. I felt a little guilty having left my new friends behind, ironically they had the same feeling and found solace moving to other places too. All was not lost and we continued to see each other at camps and events. I made new friends, and the atmosphere of the barn was pleasant with only the odd unwelcome comment here or there. It seemed they grew tired of picking on me since there were now others doing what looked like the same thing. I soon realised that in such a short time, only two years in fact, the message of this particular horse training and the fact that it had become more popular and readily available had indeed helped many people be successful with their horses.

Just like me, they had maybe struggled with them or had simply searched for another, friendlier way to train them. The unfortunate side is that like Chinese whispers the real message, technique, habits and skills had started to change and sometimes looked nothing like what I had learned at all.
This was happening not just at this barn but all over the world and the true message was dissolving or was shaped and formed and being taught in another way, resulting only in different and sometimes very bad examples. This eventually gave those that disliked and disagreed with it all a confirmation that somehow they were right. I could argue here that any training technique used by misguided or misunderstanding hands is going to be wrong, indeed I could, but everybody knows this already and to me personally there is something more important than any of that, at the end of the day we just need to ask:

"What does the animal think?"

CHAPTER 4   Part II

Listen to the horses   Persistence in an immoral world

The way I see things now is very simple, realistic and honest, and today I believe there is something very wrong with someone's education if their horse's answer to most of the things they ask them is:

"I cannot" or "I will not".

Especially if the horse is shouted and sworn at in a human language which it does not understand, and is subject to torment and abuse with the same helpless rituals over and over again; sometimes backed up by sharp welts from a whip or inflicted with cuts from over used spurs. Or are bruised and numbed from human's heels that kick the horse to move forward for so long now that it actually does not mean anything to them anymore. I do not see how anyone can have an opinion about what I do if they do anything like this to their horses. I will be the first to admit that prior to all of this I trained in some of these ways too. The difference is that I decided there was much more to horses than that, and in the process learned how to not cut corners to please my ego or tie my horse mouth shut to hide my mistakes. This is not a bitter attack towards everybody else that owns a horse and does not train the way I chose to, but it is a true fact that this does and will continue to go on until people know differently.

The forlorn part of this is that like me, many horse owners who had or are having problems with their equine friends for whatever reason either do not know they have a problem or will not admit they do, and it is usually because it is easier to just ignore it. In the last eight or so years and with humour as my intention I can tell you many examples, and one that springs to mind is of the very individuals who wilfully told me that what I was doing was very wrong or dangerous. Then somehow behind closed doors they emulated the same techniques. In these situations I will often smile inside, especially when they try to tell me later with absolute conviction that what they are doing is not the same thing. I tend to agree with that actually because it is the attitude and the understanding of the how and the why that is teaching the horse, not just the technique. A rather funny fact is that a small handful of those people who protested at the very beginning resulted later in becoming very good students of the program.

The point here is that the information they have taken on board comes from the very same source as my information did, they either genuinely do not know that or make the executive decision not to acknowledge that too. I am not the only one who found themselves in this situation, there are currently tens of thousands of us. Anyway it makes no difference, what's done is done. What interests me now is how to compensate this and one way I have learned to do that is to empower oneself and become a better example of the message. If like me you want to go the whole way and learn how to legitimately teach this way, fantastic and the more the merrier. That is exactly how I knew I wanted to teach what I was learning, I realised without a doubt that other people wanted to learn it too, some indeed already were and very well, it was the ones who were not learning it well or at all that caught my attention. Remember, it should not necessarily matter what training technique you choose to use or what sport you choose to participate in if the animal in question is healthy and happy. But I do encourage all horse owners to ask themselves two questions and be honest about what they think the answer would be:

"Am I a good teacher?"
"If my horse had a choice, would it turn up to my class the next day?"

By default horses are incredibly forgiving, some will tolerate a lot of unnecessary force and even abuse and some will do this for a lifetime. In their innocence they allow it to continue because they do not complain and in addition can make the owners feel morbidly successful. Other horses have a lower tolerance so their health will eventually deteriorate, or worse still they inflict an unnecessary injury by tearing a tendon, muscle or ligament or end up having something like a bad back. In return sometimes this can make their humans bitter, or they simply just trade in for another horse.

Then there are the others, a small majority of horses just like Mia who will say:

"No." and *"I am not having any of that."*

In return, like me the human will try to find another way that will work or usually end up quitting all together.

Let us compare a horse to a dog, you can vocally teach a dog a command that they understand almost immediately like sit, wait and fetch. They can learn and will even listen to a human's voice commands during highly stressful situations if trained well enough, like a Police dog. You can absolutely do the same with a horse, however they are called tricks simply because it is not a reliable language for them and will only happen when they are working in a safe environment. The horse cannot listen to a vocal cue when he has high adrenaline in his system and his instinct is telling him to survive or run. Remember that when a horse uses vocals it is mostly because they are stressed, feel like there is danger or are requesting some sort of confirmation. If you witness somebody telling their horse vocally to do something and then when the horse does not respond receives a punishment for it, there is something very wrong with that scenario.

A word you will hear often in the horse world, especially in sports like dressage where the horse is required to perform gymnastics, is lightness. Meaning for example that whatever we ask the horse to do, he will do with the slightest touch or suggestion. Perhaps the horse needs to be light on the forehand so that he can work better on his hind quarters, or the aids and cues get to the point where they are almost invisible. It always interests me how people who drag, push, kick, poke and trust me there are worse things that they do to their horses and then think they have the right to complain that their horses are not light. How can they be? If the horse understands what your strength is, which by the way is nothing compared to theirs, it will become their calculation of lightness. To teach horses any form of lightness you need to show them what it is you are asking of them first. For example if I ask a horse to walk on the ground next to me and he resists, he might lean on the halter and soon figure out I am not as strong as he is therefore this will become his lightness. If I ask the horse to walk and he resists and I have a way of driving him forwards without using my strength, pretty soon he can't figure out how strong I am and in return he will find the lightness. A small example, but that is all it is, having answers which do not require strong hands and human ego. Sometimes it really can just be a misunderstanding between human and horse, or a student and an instructor. A teacher may invest hours upon hours into a student's education and for whatever reason the student just does not seem to get what they are trying to teach them. Then one day the student hires another instructor who tells the student the same information but in another way, a way which resonates with them and all of a sudden they get it. It is neither the instructor nor the student's fault, it is because human beings in general tend to learn differently to each other, horses on the other hand tend to learn the same and for thousands of years that has not changed.

In 2009 I rocket launched myself into a serious and full on learning frenzy so much so that it almost got me fired from my work place at the time. Besides attending as many training events as financially possible and using most of my spare time when not with my husband to train Mia, in my breaks and during work hours in the office I would listen to the information or watch the videos on my computer. I got caught out a few times and was finally given a warning. Fortunately I was fairly good at my job, I apologised and somehow still got away with doing it. At a certain point we were also in a position where I could cut my working days down from five days a week to four days, and somehow I would still manage to use that time up to be with the horses. In 2010 it was possible for me to go to the United States of America to study and participate in a course which if I passed would qualify me to continue with further training and become a Professional. With my husband's support to spend one month away from home, I did just that. I passed the course and had qualified to do a further three month externship, which if I was good enough at the end meant I could leave there as a qualified professional. After the month away I had not actually thought that far ahead yet, so when the time came around and it became apparent that I could actually do it and would leave home for so long, I almost said no. Despite appearances it was not an easy decision to make and a lot went on behind the scenes. For a start I hated to leave my husband for so long, of course Mia too and not to mention the financial burden. Somehow we figured it out and it was made possible for me to do it, I left home in June and in September that same year returned home proudly qualified enabling me to teach everything I had learned and continue to do so to this day.

During the early days as a rookie instructor it did not take me long to recognise some important and valuable lessons, just like that old saying:
You can take a man to knowledge but you can't make him think!

It is incredibly hard to get people to understand and learn what you are teaching them, especially when a living, breathing and decision making animal is involved. It takes a certain amount of energy, conviction, talent, imagination and a ton of patience to get them to learn and want to keep on learning, plus remember it and then also be good at it. I am sure one advantage I had was my personal experience with a troubled horse and because of our situation and living circumstances we most definitely learned the hard way. Mia gave me a first-hand personal experience of what a troubled horse looked and felt like. The ones that witnessed first-hand our changes and development went out of their way then and sometimes still today to tell me, either in person or via videos and pictures they see on the internet, of just how magnificent that change was. I am always grateful for this since the past had been the absolute reverse and I always take great pleasure in helping people and giving advice from those days.

As time passed we became inseparable partners, I swear people have started to disbelieve the stories of who we used to be. Just like the American Indians we had become one. It was my grandmother who once said to me when I was very little:

"You have the spirit of the horse within you; you must learn how to embrace it."

Having become a professional I felt like I had started to keep that promise for her, and it meant that I had to return to the USA a few more times to further develop my education and experience. On one particularly memorable occasion I drove Mia back across the pond to England so we could train together with one of the founders of my education. A noteworthy experience, requiring me to trailer Mia solo for many hours including taking the ferry crossing from Calais to Dover in thick fog.

It is known for horses to have a poor short term memory and an incredibly good long term memory, and Mia showed me this as we drove down the old streets where she grew up by calling out to her old herd mates as we passed by the pastures where she used to reside. I could still remember some of them by name as they galloped over to say hello. During that trip we gave a small demonstration of what we did and why, and at the end when all was quiet Mia just stood there loose in the paddock staring out across the valley at her old home. She did this for about twenty minutes, not moving just staring and possibly thinking and digesting it all, she looked like she had when I first met her some ten years before, perfect and silent.

The beginning of 2012 started with a new family member being the presence of our new puppy, I had had the pleasure of having a dog in my life before but not while I had lived in the Netherlands, and to have one in my life again was more rewarding than words can describe. By this time I had been teaching part time for two years and could finally quit the confines of my office employment by becoming self-employed and working outside permanently. It was during those days other things became very apparent to me too. Despite having the most amazing time helping people with their horses and teaching them a different way to do things that really worked, I was and still am one of the very few trainers worldwide who does not have their own training facility. Without trying to sound ungrateful, this did not and unfortunately still does not work in my favour. I have absolutely no control over certain situations and people do unfortunately take advantage of that. I have experienced everything negative a human can inflict on you including bullying and verbal abuse and worse still, it has happened in the presence of my clients. In return I have sometimes been taken less seriously because of it, with all due respect to a certain extent not being able to control this, I am helpless. On a more positive note I refuse to let this stop me and my students progressing and because of that can't help but sometimes feel more responsible for them then I should. The owner and manager of the farm was incredibly helpful and understanding and has gone out of his way to facilitate everybody's needs.

At the risk of losing some friends with my personal critique and probably being misunderstood because it would take a whole book to really say what I mean, I am going to try and explain the following anyway.
There is unfortunately a big misconception that in order to be good with horses you need to do dressage and I am here to tell you that it simply is not the case. Personally I have a love hate

relationship with the sport because it never did me or my horses any favour in the past. Some of that was down to bad luck really, by me not being surrounded by knowledgeable enough people or by my not really listening to what they were teaching, whatever it was I grew to not be a big fan of it. That was until recently where people I admire broke down the pieces by using horsemanship and psychology to help make the sport more understandable again.

Dressage is a discipline, it is not everything. This is an important message because it is the one sport where I see humans' egos ruin the relationship with their horses the most, and it does not have to be that way. Just like the message of Natural Horsemanship, the true meaning of its origins got lost somewhere and it is time to stand up and start addressing it.

So today you will not hear me use the word *Dressage* too often. I simply refer to this discipline as gymnastics or biomechanics. The old and new masters would tell you that it takes years and years to develop both a human and a horse to a reasonable level and nothing less. Not so long ago, in the 1960's the horses who reached such high levels of gymnastics were around the age of at least twelve years old and mostly older. Today they will be four years old and are usually broken down before they even reach the age of ten years old. Please if anything may I encourage all horse enthusiasts to pay attention to this, it is destroying the sport and it is destroying what is supposed to be a beautiful thing. There are many good celebrity dressage riders out there today but unfortunately their numbers are small in comparison to the ones who are not. Some of the greatest masters taught their horses how to use their body and understand the aids from the ground first and with the support of a helper on the ground were then taught how to do the same carrying a rider. The results were and still are phenomenal and equally rewarding for all involved.

That leads me to my next point where in the early days of the way I was taught to train, not all but most people are initially required to spend a certain amount of time working with their horses from the ground first. In some cases this is for safety, for others it is to learn how to understand and work with horses better first and others because their horse really has no education and it is quite frankly dangerous to do much else. Then when they are ready they will start the next stage of riding. This being far from modern tradition is another way to raise eyebrows, but we must not forget that most of the people who come to me specifically for training have troubles with their horses and in some cases dangerous ones, and others are genuinely working on horse and/or human confidence. So from a safety point of view it is a logical requirement. It is also a specialty of mine and I am immensely proud of each and every single student who did indeed have issues and took full responsibility for it, admitted it and decided to do something about it. Friends can lose friends during this process especially with the things that I have mentioned so far. I always try to encourage people that what is lost is equally gained. At a certain time in their training when they are ready to ride it also requires us to use other facilities for their lessons like an arena. Here too unfortunately I have had to smile at unwelcome remarks, such as:

"You are not allowed in here?", or things as insulting as:
"Why are you in here? You guys don't ride."

Unfortunately people forget that what I am doing is my profession so when they talk down to me like that, they are affecting that. I would never dream of walking into their workplace to tell them how to do their job and with such an undertone. It is not my intention to make this book become a revenge tactic or a way to get back at them, it really is not, besides all of that I do not need to. We must not forget that this book is about a journey of events that leads from one to the other and in order to explain that, you need to know who I am in order to understand who Mia is. At the end of the day if my customer is happy, their horses are happy and my horses are happy, together we can stay strong and today I find myself content because it would take a lot to break that.

CHAPTER 5

The golden surprise   The beautiful golden horse

Just a few kilometres away in the next town I had been offered
the opportunity to move to another barn, and a friend of mine at
that time decided she would like to join me on that venture.
There were many positives and the main attraction was that I
could work with my horse in private, something I had secretly
been yearning for especially the past few years having been
constantly under a spotlight, even more so since it had become
my profession. Whatever I taught was generally illuminated and
it did not matter if I was working with Mia or a client and their
horse, there was always somebody who knew better who hung
around. Maybe they did, I just never saw them practice it. An
audience in passing or stopping by for a few moments to watch
will commonly see only one thing, and that unfortunately is their
perception of the negative stuff or I could say *the bumps in the
road,* and they rarely wait around long enough to see the positive
stuff or the end result.
Any seasoned professional will tell you that it is not going to be
all pretty pictures, kisses and unicorns, especially if the horse has
people problems or safety issues. It may well be an end goal for
it to look something like that ideal, but the journey there is
usually very different and that is because of the conflict between
man and horse's nature. There is a big difference between hitting
a horse and blocking one, a very big difference and to the
uneducated eye they might not see a difference, this can easily
create incorrect judgements.
Horses perceive everything as pressure and in one way or
another pressure will motivate them to move their feet, they also
have two principal emotions which are flight or fight. Another
way of saying that is to fear or dominate.

Taking these facts into consideration, it is evident that they do not share the same emotions as us, therefore it is hypocritical on our behalf for not recognising and accepting that. Their emotions are a requirement to them, they are not there to upset you or piss you off. Not to misguide the reader, there are always good moments and they far outweigh the bad, we as a whole just need to learn how to see them. If this were not true I would be out of a job, but as mentioned it is only a human's instinct to search for, register and remember the negative, so sometimes it can feel like an unwinnable battle. I have learned how to show, share and teach my students to remember that, and pretty soon the problem is over because most of the time the problem is not about the problem.

Back then, I was one of the very few people who could do pretty neat things with my horse and sometimes it was common for us to draw a crowd as we worked together, but this also happened during our learning moments. Being an innately unconfident person I found this extremely uncomfortable, and worse still people felt compelled to ask me what I was doing in these moments. It was a challenge to find a way to tell them politely that I was there to work and train with my horse and not them. Today it is so popular to work with horses this way that students are blossoming all over the world. Mia could lie down, roll over and stay on her back while I tickle her belly and nobody would take much notice, whereas a few years ago they would be in awe at such a sight. Therefore my point is that being a professional at a public barn with some one hundred and eighty horses and almost double that in humans is not exemplar for me per se, and is still the situation today.

There was nowhere else to go and one day I look forward to the mutual prospect with my husband of finding our own small farm. I have nothing to hide and learn better how to handle things every day, but it is not without its rough patches once in a while. After all I am still only human and I never signed a contract to not occasionally speak my mind.

We did move to the new location and initially it was idyllic, we shared a fenced field with four other horses and in the middle of the two acre pasture was a small lake that was split directly into two, with wire running right through the middle above the water. The small stable block was situated off a small private lane. We had a stall each and some storage areas. There was a modest yet small sand arena opposite the stable area, and I was pleased to find out that every day I had it mostly to myself with not a soul around; my introverted self-celebrated gleefully. It was possible to ride around the property and through a tiny private forest and on the other side you could also find the main yard, more stables and a lunging pen. I did not go to the main barn area often, only to fetch our hay that was stored there and stopping by sometimes to make a cup of tea on rainy or colder days.

I had a great time that summer, doing my best to progress in our riding and continuing with things that we had started, but then the winter came. It was unbelievably wet, the fields turned into one big wet stomping ground of clay and mud and not long after that, the ice followed. The lake had frozen so they had to switch off the water pipes in case they burst, which meant we had to ice pick the lake for drinking water. If we were lucky it was possible to fetch water from the main barn and in worst case scenarios I had to bring it from home. It was a lot of hard work and I found myself spending more time taking care of the horses than I actually did anything with Mia, not such a bad thing I suppose but to add to the frustration there was no electricity at our end of the property and it meant that my friend could only work with her horse during the weekends, it was then that we reluctantly decided to look for another place.

Earlier that same year in 2012 I had been visiting a friend to give advice and to help her tame two wild Connemara colts she had imported from Ireland. I had not stepped out of my car yet when one of them really caught my attention, there was something about the little guy that just captured my heart. I was not looking for another horse, I meet between four and eight horses a day and the thought had not occurred to me, but there he was. He seemed so familiar, like we had known each other before or something like that, of course we hadn't but I knew there and then I had to find a way to buy him. Across the pasture were the two punky little dudes, one a roan which is a brown and grey colour called Jonny and the other a dun which means a blonde coat with a black mane and tail, called Kheelen. We could not do too much with them the first lesson, but she was doing a fantastic job already and I left her with my advice and some things to do to help the taming process continue. As I left I could not help but smile inside followed by my heart skipping a beat or two at the thought of maybe not seeing him again. Thankfully she did call again for another lesson and I could not wait to get back there and see him. She had done everything I had taught her plus a whole bunch more, all in the favour of taming the two fellows. I was honoured too since as soon as I got out of my car he came over to greet me at the gate. She smiled and said:

"You two are cute together!"

And before I could control what was in my head, my mouth blurted out:

"You know if you ever decide to sell him please think of me first."

A few weeks later she texted me to say he was indeed for sale and again in my haste and desire to have him I made an instant deal. The funny thing was, I had not mentioned it to my husband yet, well the buying part anyway, he sure had heard about the little golden horse because I had not stopped talking about him, but he had no idea I had put a deposit on him, or so I thought. We made a deal that if she could keep him for that summer I would be able to pay for him with lessons and deposits of money when I had it, a kind gesture she willingly accepted and I am forever grateful for. Early that winter we went for a small vacation in the sun and me being me just could not get the idea out of my head how to tell Jort, of course he knew and had already figured everything out.

One night during a romantic candlelit dinner at an enchanting harbour, completely out of the blue he said:

"You know that little horse you do not stop talking about?"

"Yes." I responded with a blush.

"Go ahead and buy him!"

And then he joked: *"Do it quickly before I change my mind."*

Now I have to sympathise with the surrounding people seated quietly at their tables on such a beautiful night because I burst into tears and whilst snuffling like a baby I jumped to my feet to kiss him all over his face while saying thank you a hundred times. Once the joy and initial shock had passed I sat back in my seat and could not stop happily sobbing. The poor waiter approached obviously embarrassed and who must have thought that Jort made me cry in another way. As he asked hesitantly what we would like to drink I started to giggle through my snotty nose and said:

"Don't worry these are happy tears, he just bought me a horse."

I had arranged to collect Kheelen also known as Lenny the first week of 2013, but found out that the weather was going to be bad with snow so arranged to pick him up during the last week of that December. A few weeks into the New Year the winter had become almost unbearable so we decided to move the horses to another place sooner than initially planned.

We had been pondering over another barn some ten kilometres in the opposite direction of home, where it was possible to have a large stable each in a nice big airy barn with our own small pasture, which we could do with what we liked. It had the added bonus of a race track, a brand new arena with bright lights and heating in the tea room, it was so much better than what we had at that time, we could not say no.

It was okay at first, the work to take care of the horses was in fact much harder especially since I now had two of them, and although we could offer them a bit of a better life it never felt like home and was becoming incredibly expensive. Poor Kheelen having moved home not once but twice in such a short time had caught himself a bit of a cold, probably related to the stress of it all and run up some very expensive vets bills to get his temperature down. Things were indeed a bit down in the dumps and I found myself having an extra hard time because I was starting to have that feeling of tiredness and self-doubt again. I dared not admit it to anyone especially Jort, since he had been so great in allowing me to buy this beautiful horse and finances were already tight.

Being self-employed, if you do not work you do not get paid so I just kept somehow powering on, it was a bad idea, I was experiencing the first phase of another burnout.

What did help for a little while was Kheelen making a full recovery and somehow we got through the first snowy months of that year. We even managed to work with the horses a bit in the arena or around the racetrack. It was a rewarding time too because some thirteen years later I was going through the same process I had with Mia but with Kheelen and with a whole bunch more knowledge. The things that took me quite possibly months back then was now taking me just a few days or less. As spring approached we were pretty much done with the place, and to add fuel to the fire I had to leave my dog in the car every day because a guard dog roamed the premises that actually killed little dogs. This was not the life for us and I could certainly not continue like that into the following summer, so we decided to ask the manager of the original barn in the natural setting if we could come back yet again, and much to our delight he said:

"Yes of course."

CHAPTER 6   Part I

White noise   The first fracture, unthinkable

If we are to talk about the way I felt on that fateful day when the veterinarian explained the result of her x-rays, it was like I was drowning and as the realisation of what he had said started to kick in I could not breathe.

It was a dark and cool room, Mia was standing quietly in the stock having been sedated to have the pictures taken and her eyes although soft, showed an unspoken concern. He invited me to step into a small side room where the x-rays were displayed on a computer screen. As I walked away, Mia shuffled as if to come with me and an assistant who had been there the whole time stayed to comfort her while I went and listened to his findings. I had heard what he said but not really, because a high pitched noise took over my internal hearing and as the words left his mouth my senses felt faint resulting in a fuzzy vision, a bit like television static. As he continued to speak, a voice in the back of my mind repetitively asked:

Broken? I cannot believe it is broken!

That is why this chapter is named: *White noise.*

With high spirits and excitement we had moved back to the former barn, the pastures were still closed for the winter and would open again in a few weeks, so we had agreed it was best to keep the horses isolated on a sand paddock and reintroduce them to the herd when that day came. It was nice to be there yet again, furthermore having extra time on my hands I could rest a little which helped my emotional state. I could also start to do something which was very important to me again and that was to put valuable time back into the relationships with my horses, and this time I did not care if it was with or without an audience. Mia looked very well, fairly slim for her usual self and showed energy in her contentment, being back on her old turf. Although we had not been away long, only seven months actually, it felt much longer and again the atmosphere seemed to have somehow changed for the better. Not yet having storage for our equipment we used my trailer, and were happy that the horses were living outside and on a dry sandy paddock.

Regrettably it was at this point Mia started to get problems and I will tell you now there are several scenarios as to what I think happened, all I can do is share the facts. It took me about two years to let it go and just come to terms with the fact that I will probably never know the whole truth, but one thing I know for sure is that I will never let something like this happen again, and hopefully by sharing this story it will help somebody else too.

It all started with her left hind heel, she got a small rash which looked like a common skin infection known in the horse world as mud fever, or in Dutch it is known as 'mok'. A minor complaint if taken care of quickly which ironically horses can get not just standing in mud and wet conditions but also in dry weather conditions. I administered your usual standard treatments for this complaint which are available over the counter in most tack stores, and it started to clear up after about four days. On day five I was horrified to discover it had come back with a vengeance, it was suddenly weeping and very sore to the touch. Not looking like mud fever anymore I had no choice but to call the vet, he diagnosed it could be a bacterial infection but since he could not touch her to really examine it, he could not be sure. He gave me some ointment and an oral medication to help it pass, and a week later although it hadn't got worse it hadn't got much better either, having only dried up a little with less weeping. After another visit from the vet, he prescribed a steroid based cream which did the trick in just a few days. I was super relieved for my sweet girl and proceeded to gently build up her training again only to find one morning she was extremely crippled on the same leg, so much so that she could not walk without what

111

was obviously chronic pain. I hoped for a hoof abscess because just like her first one, as ugly and painful as they can be they are usually curable. The vet came to visit yet again and confirmed what I had thought, it was a hoof abscess. I performed the usual ritual for this particular problem including soaking her hoof at least twice a day, three when possible, keeping the hoof clean, followed by monitoring her temperature. On day two I saw a hole in the hoof where the pus had eventually made its way out and after a quick follow up visit with the vet he confirmed another standard practice for this problem, and that was to keep the exit wound open so the rest of the infection could drain out. Much to our relief on day five it was over, I was extremely happy for her since that weekend the pastures would open and she could run free in the grass again with her friends.

The weekend came and passed, for me there is no better sound than walking past a field and hearing the gentle swish of a horse's tail to wipe away a spring fly and hearing the comical munch of their teeth as they eat the lush grass. Both my horses appeared happy, as was I since I had plans to go away for a family weekend soon and just wanted her to be well. Around that time I had befriended a girl, she had a big place in her heart for Mia and we made an agreement which suited us both for her to part share her. It was perfect timing since I now had two horses and money was still tight especially after so many vets' bills, it was a great help indeed. It was also the beginning of a new chapter for us, Mia having been so particular about people accepted her and they got along famously, and that was all that mattered. What sold me was her openness and honesty, of course she worked the same way as I did and to quite a sufficient level, a perfect match. I had been thinking about it for quite some time especially since that old problem was still there haunting us where Mia had zero tolerance for veterinarians and certain types of people. It made sense to start the process of having other people in her life and ones we trusted. I realised she needed it and I have to say it was not an easy decision to make, nonetheless it was a good one. The family weekend came around and on the Friday before we left, I saw Mia move around on the field, she was not crippled but she was not one hundred percent right either. Sometimes she looked okay and other moments not, so I made a deal with her and the universe that I would give her the weekend to get better and if she was still the same when I got back I would call the vet again.

Now the veterinarian practice or clinic as it can also be referred to that I had been using, although reputable and of course good at their job just did not sit right when it came to Mia and I, so when I came home to find her the same still, I called a different practice. A female doctor arrived and Mia whom had not let any of the three vets from the other practice touch her, actually let this young lady touch and examine her straight away and as you can imagine after thirteen years I was very impressed. She diagnosed that the infection from the hoof abscess was not drained completely, and that it was best to put her on a four to six day treatment plan again to clean and help the hoof drain. I might add here that Mia also allowed her to re-open the original exit wound, a painful situation and one the mare did not fight.

I had to keep her on the sand paddock again and since the horses were all out to pasture decided to put Kheelen there too to keep her company, memories of that broken nose the first time she had an abscess never left my mind so I did not want her in a stable for this. The vet left me with my orders which as per usual I executed with duty and perfectionism, and the rest of the days I went about my business training Kheelen and teaching my students. On day four, a small amount of pus finally decided to exit into the warm bucket of water I soaked her hoof in, and the next day she walked much better again. With permission from the vet, we agreed she could go back to the pasture and I was to just monitor her at least for a few days before reintroducing her training.

It was now mid-May, and one morning as I walked my dog close to the pastures I could see Mia acting unusually restless, this was so unlike her it got my immediate attention. The horse that never

113

ran for spontaneous fun, not since she was a youngster anyway, never groomed with other horses let alone play with them was now running up and down the fence line as though her life depended on it. During that time it was possible to have your horse on a pasture, and when the horses moved to a new one with fresh grass you could leave your horse on the original pasture so as to limit the grass intake, and then release them into the new pasture a few days later because the other horses would have eaten the new grass down. I had done this before so it was nothing new, except this day a mare she had buddied with was in the new pasture and Mia was evidently upset that she was not with her. It was one of those weeks where all the mares came into heat together, Mia will always show a bit more interest in other horses during these times, sometimes allowing them to stand next to her and in her space, but I had never seen her obsessed with another horse like this before. I still had one last lesson to teach that day and made an on the spot decision that I would check on her when the hour was over and if she was still the same I would just let her in the new field. I came back to find her agitated and a bit sweaty and although she was not running up and down the fence like a lunatic anymore she was obviously still very stressed. When I called her she came running, this was something Mia would only do when she was hungry or wanted something and in this case she was asking for both. I could not face the prospect of another vet bill so I decided to let her through to the new field where of course she found her friend and all was forgotten, kind of.

The next day I was very disappointed to find she was slightly lame again, not super sore but something was definitely not right, all my concerns had come true, I called the vet and she came to examine her once more, only this time her prognosis was a little different. She said something along the lines of:

"She walks and looks like she has an abscess but something in her movement tells me differently."

We agreed to continue and treat the abscess, and if it was not better in two days I was to take her to the veterinary practice for further examination. Slightly relieved at also finding out they had a stock too, I was happy we had a new plan. It was here things went terribly wrong. Mia did not want to be in the sand paddock anymore, its only view was that of the pasture where all of her herd and new girlfriend were standing. I put Kheelen there again too to keep her company and it was as if he was not there, she just kept calling and running up and down in the sand, which was much deeper now since we had had a dry period, and her turns and twists made me cringe. I called the vet and told her the situation, I was certain that if she went back to her friend she would rest better than this, after all, she does not play, she does not tend to run etc. The vet agreed and with adrenaline still in her system I knew better than to just let her go as soon as we got through the gate, so I walked her across the field to her friend before setting her loose in the hope that she would settle straight away. It worked a treat and within moments of greeting her friend she had her nose in the grass. Naturally I felt some relief, but also apprehension about the situation. I was sure she would be calmer and more content like this, and whatever the problem was she would do more harm by staying in the deep sand than out there on the flat grass land. I drove back again quite late that evening to check on her and found her happily eating with her head in the grass; stupidly, I do not recall actually seeing her move around. The next morning, I had just made my coffee, it must have been seven o'clock and my phone rang, a young man who kept his horse at the barn happened to be riding past the field on his way to the dunes and he saw what he could only describe as:

"Mia is standing on three legs, it does not look good."

I asked: *"Left hind?"*

He responded: *"Afraid so."*

I jumped in my car, drove reasonably fast a fraction over the speed limit where possible to get to the barn, grabbed my halter from the trailer and ran as fast as could to the very back of the field, where she was now standing with her friend who was not too far away snoozing. I could see she rested the left hind leg and could see no obvious damage or cuts. I figured the best thing to do was to get her down to the main barn area and go from there. Once her halter was on I asked her to take a step forwards. Of course she resisted, with all our training and my experience to date I knew the feel of that type of resistance now and it did not come from a place of *I will not,* like it had sometimes in the past, it came from a place of *I cannot*.

Inside my heart started to thump, I knew this was not good, her stomach muscles were tense and tight and she had a look of pain in her eyes I had not seen before, my darling Mia was hurting beyond words and I felt so incredibly helpless. The first thought I had was to call the vet, I told them my situation and they asked me to do my best to get her back to the barn and that they would meet us there. Realising I could not do this alone, using my phone I called around for people who would still be at the barn around that time of the day for urgent help. I knew some of the regulars who could still be there and after a few phone calls three people came as quick as they could. We proceeded to walk Mia together step by painstaking step, it was about half a kilometre to get across the fields and down the sand track back to the main barn area, it felt like twenty. It took us forty minutes and that felt a lot longer too. I have never in my life seen a horse walk the way she did, or one who had figured out a way to walk to alleviate pain.

After a few meters evidently she had figured out that we were heading towards the barn and with too much to think about she did not look back for her friend, but did start to aid us in helping her get there. She decided of her own free will that if she walked sideways to the left she did not have to put all her weight on that left hind leg so we let her do just that. Everybody was great and it melted my heart to see Mia let strange hands touch her, and the way she listened and trusted their support. After a few more meters I had to look twice, a kind of double take if you will, because as she settled slowly into this sideways walk I saw her leg swing at a funny and very abnormal angle forwards and sideways before it went back to the ground again. It was like her leg was disconnected. Swallowing hard and trying not to cry, I focused on the job at hand to get her back to the barn where in perfect time we met the vet. She saw us walk the last few steps, and as our eyes met she gave a few comforting words and said:

"I will see you there!" meaning the veterinary practice.

She jumped in her car and while somebody held and comforted Mia, I hitched up my trailer and parked it as close to her as I could. I remember I was very angry at myself those last moments, thinking why did we not take the trailer to the field and bring her down like that. In my defence and in a bid to quit torturing myself I will say, how were we to know? You do what you have to do in those moments and if it was not for that I may not have seen the swinging leg, never in any of our thoughts did we want to believe her leg was actually broken.

Mia who by now was a trailer loading pro, proceeded to walk herself in and allowed me to help lift her hind leg up the ramp step-by-step; naturally an audience had accumulated, news had travelled fast. Much to my surprise they offered no unwelcome advice and were only star struck by what they were witnessing, and my horse's willingness to oblige and try her best in such a nightmarish situation. Once settled, I drove the very short distance which usually took about fifteen minutes in about twenty five, to keep the journey safe and comfortable for my dear friend.

One of the girls who witnessed the whole thing had made two signs saying *SICK HORSE* in Dutch and by using duct tape stuck them in clear view on the front and the back of the trailer. I can't tell you how helpful it was because drivers really respected that sign. On areas where the road was open and cars would usually overtake *that no good slow horse trailer,* they actually waited

117

and as we had to turn over a small bridge and down some very narrow streets in the nearby village, cars moved right out of their way to let us through. It was an elating feeling in such a situation, not forgetting to mention I was on my own. The people who helped us at the barn had to go to work or take care of their children, but I had some comfort because the drive was fairly short and the vet was waiting for me at the other end, two of them in fact. It was the first time I was to meet a particular vet, who having followed in his father's footsteps was now the head vet of this practice. I was very pleased to finally meet him and see that he was there to help.

I unloaded Mia the only way we could, which was backwards and very slowly. I let her figure the way out herself and helped her lift her leg when she needed. Once unloaded we proceeded to walk the very short distance to the examination room, where he watched intently without saying a word about the way she moved; the female vet who visited earlier had already brought him up to speed. He invited me to walk Mia into the examination room and put her into the stock, and it was here she finally said:

"No, I do not want to."

It gave me a small glimpse of hope, she had a lot of fight left in her yet, the vet offered to help and I responded:

"Please can you just give me a few minutes and she will be fine."

I have to say I was very happy to find he respected my wishes, after all this was a man with much experience, and having more than likely seen horses do this every day he could have easily offered his own solutions to help, but he did as I asked and of course a few minutes later she was in. No easy feat, she had to enter the room and then manoeuvre sideways to stand in the stock, but she had to move sideways to the right. Thank goodness for all my ground work and bonding skills, had we not trained this way I do not know how we would ever have got her in there without a battle, the thought can still give me nightmares.

The smell of alcohol and cleaning detergent dominated the room and I could see that look in Mia's eyes, the one where she is deathly terrified and could lash out in defence at any moment, or not. The head vet introduced himself officially and managed to touch Mia, she responded with a tense jerk, I would not necessarily say it was towards him, just tense. After questioning me and collecting additional facts, much to my relief he concluded it was best to sedate her, and that he would take several x-rays from hip to hoof to find out what was really going on. It was a memorable conversation, he already kind of knew what could be wrong, there was something in his tone that gave that away, I admire that he did not second guess anything until the evidence was available.

In front of the stock where Mia was standing and about a meter away stood a small desk area with a drugs cabinet; from there any horse could clearly see what was going on, especially a horse like Mia who was convinced her very life depended on it. As he prepared the hypodermic needle and alcohol swab, by her body language alone and his experience he could already tell that she had past trauma. In the midst of my concerns and a huge headache, which now blackened the corners of my eyes I somehow managed to be impressed. He proceeded to tell me he knew of many horses with troubles like this, and of only one other horse that was this sensitive and that had been years ago when his father was in practice.

With that said he won my trust immediately, he did not blame her, he just acknowledged her. Mia was hyper alert, all of her survival instinct and sensory systems were in overdrive, I think the adrenaline in her system was at an all-time high and she made quite the fuss about having the needle. I cannot and will never blame her for that, everything to her was strange and scary, her instinct knew with a hurting leg she was now on the food chain. I had also transported her to the one place she hated the

most in the world, and had to convince her to go in a small room with low lighting and stand in the stock, or you could say trap, while she was injected in the neck only to be rendered helpless. She had every right to be afraid and pissed off and if there was any other way to do this, I would have, but there was not.
He gave her a larger than normal dose, knowing we would be there for quite some time and disappeared into his little side room while the effects of the drug started to do its work. Left alone I stood with her, in some kind of incognito state, with heavy tears I swallowed hard as I stroked her beautiful face and pitifully told her, whatever it was:

"I am sorry, I am so very sorry."

Before long she was under sedation and her head dropped lower and lower into my arms as the effect got stronger. The ten minutes passed and he appeared with an assistant who helped prepare us for the x-rays. Standard protocol requires you to wear a lead based apron, we all put one on before they proceeded to set up and move the machine, which was fixed to the ceiling, into position for the pictures. As promised he took as many x-rays as required from hip to hoof. Mia stood quietly the whole time, just dozing with her heavy head in my arms, at one point I had pins and needles and could not feel them anymore but I could not let her go, I did not want to.
A man of few words at this time he vanished again into his little side room. It felt like forever while he examined the pictures, having left myself and Mia in the dark room busy with our thoughts. He returned to ask for permission to take two more pictures of her knee but this time from another angle, he thought he could see something and this angle would help determine his diagnosis. They set up the machine again accept this time and much to my surprise Mia stirred a little in her drugged sleep, she could feel the x-ray machine was going into another position. The knee of a horse in the hind leg is high up, it is actually the front joint where it connects to the main body behind the belly area, so the x-ray plate which was held on a T shaped board had

to go behind her knee, and between both of her back legs. Within a tenth of second of the board being held in that location, she kicked, and not only did she kick hard she did it with the injured leg and she did not miss. The board flew out of the assistant's hand and to say I was shocked is an understatement I thought: *How the hell did she do that?*

The atmosphere in the room immediately changed, he looked at me with reassurance and in such a way that I knew this was certainly not anything new to him, but his look also told me that this was it, this was the place and something was very wrong. My legs were like jelly, he proceeded politely to continue and whenever Mia showed signs of concern he burst into an unexpected song where his Dutch accent would suddenly fill the room with a pleasant version of Frank Sinatra's New York, New York.
Believe me when I say this helped not just Mia but everybody in the room relax and before long he had taken the two x-rays and disappeared back to his side room again. The vet assistant and I exchanged a few glances, acknowledging that it was indeed something special, and again we waited.
It was here he called me into the room to look at the pictures on the computer screen while he explained his findings.

After my initial shock of white noise, I had to ask him to repeat again what he said, I just could not comprehend the worst nightmare of all horse owners was being told to me right there and in that moment. I almost fell over, my jelly legs were now stiff as I walked the few steps back to her. I wrapped my arms around her head as if to protect her and my body language had gone into an automatic defence mode. Still having not really heard a word he said, my mind clearly started to react at the now new thoughts screaming in my ears: *She is going to die, oh my god she is going to have to be put down to sleep and die, not here, please if anything NOT HERE!*

The broken bone was indeed very severe, she had fractured off a part of the tibia which in human terms is the top of your shin bone, the part that sticks out right below your knee.
That section of bone is where the patellar ligament attaches and is the structure that holds your patella in place, so by fracturing the bone in the way she did she had completely destabilized her knee. The worse part was that because of the way horses move, there is a constant upward force being exerted on the patellar tendon with every step they take, making it very difficult to heal.

Terrified about what he was about to say and what we were going to do next, I became incredibly possessive, like a mother protecting her child, nobody was going to take her away from me, not like this and not yet. The overdue credit I want to give him really starts now, he could see what I was thinking, he knew right away that this was going to be no easy task and with very few words he came up with a temporary solution.

In so many words he said:

"Take her home and put her in a stable, a small one, she must not move around too much. I will do some research and will call you back within twenty four hours, and we will see what we can do."

With a shaky hand I shook his and we slowly made our way home. I have to be honest here when I say I do not remember that trip home, none of it. With all due respect I should not have been driving and in hindsight it was irresponsible. Thankfully in my shocked state we made it back to the barn, and as soon as I parked the car and trailer and pulled up the handbrake I burst into a surge of heartbroken tears, and did not stop for a very long time.

At a certain point I got myself together and called the barn manager to tell him the situation and that I needed a stable for Mia. He kindly gave us one located in a place where she could see other horses when they were in the barn area and not out onto the actual pastures, still not ideal since she was on her own, but it was what he could offer at that time. That evening after the sedation had worn off the adrenaline in her body did not dissipate, despite being in what must have been immense pain, all her focus was again being back with the safety of her herd. It reminded me how intense her willpower was, and how right now it did not matter what I did, it was too late. I decided that to get her through the next twenty four hours without hurting her nose on the top of the door again or worse still kill herself, that I would give some oral sedative to quieten her down. It helped some, and although she would eat her hay over the door to look for the other horses she was mostly quiet, and once the adrenaline left her system much to my relief she finally stood there in her innocent quietness and slept.

CHAPTER 6   Part II

You might be lucky   Some expectations

I will never forget the next day; while Mia was eating fairly content in her stable I was busy trying to teach a student and her friend who had come to spectate. About ten, maybe fifteen minutes into the lesson my phone rang. I had explained in advance that I was expecting a call about Mia and when it rang I had to take it. He told me what he had to tell me, and as I heard his words my knees folded underneath me as I fell to the ground. The ladies in question knew some of the story but not all of it, I had not told many people her leg was actually broken yet because I did not want to deal with the fuss. I did not want, and could not handle everybody asking me all day what had happened and having to repeat myself over and over. Not yet anyway, not until I had all the facts. It sounds selfish but that was the way I felt.

In a bundle of tears, I gave the ladies a quick version of the whole story and gave my apologies that I could not finish the lesson. They looked at me with pity, having not quite grasped the situation themselves, and naturally agreed. I ran back to Mia's stable, opened the door and just hugged her. I hugged her for so long my arms ached; that moment was so incredibly heart breaking, I completely lost track of time.

The vet had told me in his research he had sent the x-rays to some of his colleagues at other veterinary practices around the country for their opinion, and they all concluded the same thing. The fracture in the knee was very unusual, so unusual in fact that they did not quite know how to treat it, and if they did treat it the outcome was also new territory. They came up with three options, all of which believe it or not brought some delight to my ears because they did not involve a gun, yet. The first option was to operate, the second was to wait three months for it to heal a little and then operate, and the third option was to let her rest for three months, repeat the x-rays to make sure it was healing well enough and if it was, the plan was to let her have all the time she needed for it to heal itself, which would be a minimum of one year, maybe two. I wanted to know all of the details of all of the options and of course all the pros and cons. He was very honest with me, and after a forty minute phone call was somewhat relieved to hear that I had chosen the last option. The operation carried big risks, not forgetting to mention the aftercare, and it had no guarantee of success. She would also have needed to be anaesthetised, and the post-operative care in particular for this one horse would have been nothing short of a nightmare, for her and everyone involved.

His parting words said:

"The bone must heal, and if there is further contusion or if scar tissue forms between the healing fractures, then you must be prepared for the worst. I wish you both all the best, you might be lucky."

As soon as the phone call was over I collected my thoughts, and then arranged to meet the barn manager to explain the situation and Mia's new, but strict instructions. She was to stay in the stable for the next three months and she was to rest and relax as much as possible. No pain killer could be administered, as cruel as that sounds it helps horses in these situations to understand they are hurt and can encourage them to rest. I was then to take her back to the veterinary clinic for further x-rays to make sure she was healing correctly.

So it was here it all started, the long road to recovery. During those initial days I had so many new and horrible emotions, I had become some sort of walking zombie. I could not sleep for worrying that she would hurt herself again; I could not eat because my stomach felt nauseous all the time and my poor sweet girl was deteriorating right before my eyes. I could not help but get upset when I was around her; she was so beautiful, so I questioned myself and the universe constantly: *How and why was this happening to her?*

On day three I noticed she had started to lose muscle mass on her quarters and so soon into the rest period, I could not imagine how she would look if we got through this. Anyhow it did not matter, as long as she lived we could get all of that back and the main thing from then on was to concentrate on each day as it came. That was eventually the answer I gave people when they asked.

Unluckily for me, I started to have that feeling yet again, the burnout was sitting deep somewhere dark in my soul, waiting to pounce like a vampire on his victim. It had gone away the first month we had moved back to the barn, even with Mia's hoof abscess issues and everything else going on it had subsided, but now it was back secretly clouding the darkest corners of my mind. I felt extremely tired and unmotivated, was short in temper at minor things and incredibly intolerant for idle talk; actual talking was such a big effort anyway, so because of that I told no one and only spoke of Mia when really necessary.

The next few days I started to notice Mia's emotions and physical appearance change too. Her eyes started to look small and dull, her coat lost its shine and despite having as much hay as she could eat she lost weight rapidly, she had become a zombie too. Then it hit me! - This poor horse was mirroring my emotions. I had been so sad, feeling sorry for myself and her, it was all so very depressing and how could she not feel that?

The next day was a Monday, I remember waking up and telling myself:

"From this day forth there will be no more sadness and feeling sorry for her or yourself! You are going to go to the barn as though nothing has happened and be happy around that horse if

126

it is the last thing you do, and you are going to go out of your way to make sure everybody else does the same."

True to my word I arrived at the barn obviously chirpier than I had been the previous days, and went about my daily chores including teaching. In between it all I made sure Mia knew she was the apple of my eye, and most important that she was going to be okay. By that afternoon her appearance had already changed, her eyes started to sparkle again and the shine in her coat had started to flourish. I am not saying we had some kind of E.T. moment or I that have extra magic powers that controlled my horse's mind, but what I am telling you is that you are your horse's environment. Ironically I had seen it so often before with other horses and their humans, that is how I came to that conclusion. If your horse or animal has an illness or is sick and you treat them like they are ill or sick, you have a high probability that they will stay sick or get sick again. Just like us, they will cope much better in a positive environment rather than a negative one. In my years around them I have seen horses that had the most awful and painful wounds, yet they went through the healing process much quicker than anticipated because of the optimism that poured out of their humans, and I have also witnessed the opposite. I did not want to be in a negative trap like that. In some sense it felt like it had been that way for a while anyway, simply because of Kheelen being sick and then Mia's rash, then her hoof abscess and then the broken bone, how can one not question themselves?
The powers that be had challenged us enough already, we needed a break so I dug deep, found the light and started to fight.

The storm before the calm   Life or death, take your pick

That summer was very warm with little rain and too many flies, it was incredibly hard to see her stuck inside the stable like that. I could only just bare it on some days, especially since she could not leave its confinement not even for a small walk; her very life depended on it. As the first weeks progressed, I could only mull over the situation, daring not to stay there too long in my thoughts or I would drive myself insane with that one big question burning in my brain: *How did she break her leg?* The various conclusions I have come to live with are as follows:

I think the mok like rash had nothing to do with it; the hoof abscess may have been an early indication that something was already broken inside, or it may have been the cause of the break by a misstep during a painful moment, and most likely happened on the evening she wanted to be in the next field with the lush new grass and her herd mate. Another scenario is that she perhaps twisted and turned too hard in the deep sand in the paddock, during her hoof abscess period. It was also possible that the fracture could have happened much earlier and got worse over time, the bugger is I will never really know.

We settled into a doable routine, I started to accept help from the kind of people Mia warmed to and as the news spread about her situation she received many loving visitors during the day and early evening. The stable was cleaned by the barn management once in the morning during the week days, and I had to do it myself in the evenings and at the weekends. As always she had ad-lib hay and help against the irritating and constant swarm of flies. One of the horse owners kindly let me use the stable next door as a temporary storage for the things she needed and we just dealt with each day as it arrived. The barn itself can be a busy place during weekends and school holidays, and although she was not housed in one of the main barn areas, she was situated at a place where people walk and pass by with their horses to get from A to B. Having a hard time relaxing even on the cooler days, I had no choice but to give her the oral drug again to help keep her slightly sedated. With everything I had learned the last few years about horses the idea of doing this sent shivers down my spine, I hated doing it but I knew with some certainty it was for her well-being at that particular time.

One afternoon my best friend who was over visiting from England came with me to take care of Mia. We arrived at the barn to find her relaxing softly in the shade of the big trees that canopied the stables. She had not been lying down often, it was very difficult for her to get up and I should imagine must have been unbearably painful. We left her for a while to take my dog for a walk and when we came back we found her to be laying down snoozing in and out of a sleep. Another moment I shall never forget simply because of how exhausted she looked, so tired barely able to keep her head up, everything about her screamed she needed more rest. It was starting to become apparent that the type of rest she needed, if she was going to need a year or more to get better, was not going to happen there. We walked away again to let her rest when all of a sudden there was a big loud crumbling bang, I looked back to see that the open area behind her stable where sometimes trucks would pull in for deliveries or take away the manure heap happened to be unloading something which made a loud rumble when it hit the floor.
My immediate words were:

"Shit, Mia"!

Looking at each other with twinned concern, fast but calmly we ran back to her stable in time to see the poor horse struggle not once, not twice but three times to her feet. Her leg just would not hold her weight and each time she tried to stand up it just gave out under her. She started to panic, and as she panicked the straw bedding on the floor had started to move aside in unhelpful clumps and expose the damp and slippery concrete floor underneath. Finally she stood up and as she did she kind of jumped as if wanting to run away from the noise that had happened over a minute ago already, and as she did she fell down again in a horrible twist and jolt, it was horrific. We were helpless for her and it felt like for a moment there she was going to die. With my face in my hands I wanted to cry out for her to stop, my heart ripped clean in two pieces thinking the same had now happened to her leg. With some composure, I opened the stable door in a bid to help her and as I was about to enter she manged to get up and immediately shook herself off. Temporarily we were dumbfounded at what we had just witnessed in that last moment. She had used only her right hind leg to heave herself up. Sitting upright like a dog, she had switched her buttocks from left to right before raising the rest of her body.

We had observed her learn something; she had found a way to cope with the broken leg and somehow in her discovery it made her remarkably calm. To lie down, horses will drop gently to their front knees first before lowering their hind quarters to the ground over their hind legs, either to the right or to the left. To get up they need to rise onto the front legs and then use their hind legs to push themselves up. That means in one moment nearly all of their bodyweight is balanced on both of their hind legs, she had just manged to do that on one leg. From that day forth I did see her lay down more often and when she got up I observed that she had perfected the art of rising on her right hind leg. A little voice in the back of my head carried some concern for this, worrying it might damage her good hind leg, but it was a little voice soon outweighed by other events that interrupted her healing time.

The first month of finding a routine and people who could help so I could continue my work schedule went fairly easily, all thanks to them. Plus learning to live with the constant and anxious worry went by surprisingly fast too. Other hurdles we had to tackle were things like more deliveries with loud noises, children and the occasional loose horse. All the kind of things you would normally expect to find at a busy equestrian farm, except now they were illuminated because my dear friend's very life depended on it. Every year the barn sanitises all of the living areas with a high pressure water hose, this too was something we had to find a way to deal with and get through.

One of the hardest parts about that whole time was getting certain people to understand that she was indeed in a life or death situation. I do not know why some people did not take it seriously, maybe they did not know all of the facts, maybe they were ignorant, after all it was *just* a horse, or maybe they just did not care. The point is, I cared and many other people did too. Much was out of my control and I could have easily broken down at any moment.

I made an agreement with the manager that they would sanitise the stable block of four where she was housed on the morning I took her to the vets for the check-up x-ray, it would then be empty for at least a few hours so they could do it then. I already knew when I made that agreement that if I could arrange it, and if I could find a way and somewhere else for her to live, she would not be coming back, not to live like that anyway. It was not for their lack of trying, it was a helpless situation presented to all of us and I could not expect them to stop all business and workload because my horse had a problem.

In my efforts to help her as much as possible, I placed three big orange traffic cones outside her stable door so people could not walk by her door too fast or too close as they passed by, spooking her in the process and causing her to jump on the broken leg. In chalk on the stable door clear for everyone to see, I wrote clearly in the Dutch language:

24/7 box rest. BROKEN LEG, must rest, and my telephone number.
These things I wish I did not have to do really since it was obvious by then that the horse was in bad shape, rumours after all travelled fast. I had to do what I had to do, and some people still misunderstood or ignored the message. One morning, unfortunately with no warning or so much as a hello, somebody asked me right out of the blue: *"Who do you think you are?"*

Shocked at the shallow and disarming question I responded with sarcasm:

"I don't know, who do you think I am?"

Looking at me with such a stare it made me feel guilty, like a police car can when they pull up behind you at the traffic lights, they responded: - *"All of this, what is this?"*

"Did you read the message on the door?"

"Yes, but it cannot be that serious, is it necessary all of this stuff?"

I responded: *"What stuff?"*

"The cones, they are in everybody's way."

As you can well imagine I had to restrain myself, if I am honest I can tell you I wanted nothing more than to knock the sarcasm out of their head. My patience was at boiling point, which they could now see was written all over my face. An apology would have been very welcome, unfortunately their pride said no and they were indecisively strong willed in the matter. I took the biggest of big breaths and did my best to kindly and unnecessarily explain that there was still a clear five meter space remaining that people could use to effortlessly walk by, the only difference was that it was not directly on the concrete ground that the stall block was built on, but was on a path next to it on dry, clean and soft sand. Of course they found fault in that too, and even had the audacity to pick on some other things, all in the bid to make their argument valid. In an effort to banish a conversation that had now gone on for way too long, I found a way inside to end it by asking their own question back again, and said:

"With all due respect, who do YOU think YOU ARE? I am just trying to do the best to make my horse as comfortable as possible with the resources I have, so that she might have a chance to get through this. What is the real problem here, can you please tell me?"

As I said it, it dawned in me, it was not about the situation, it was not about Mia, it was not about anything, it was only about them, and it usually always is in these types of circumstances. I had not realised it sooner, because I was still recovering from the agonising suggestions. My tone had been firm but not mean, and with that they sympathetically responded:

"I'm sorry, I didn't realise it was so bad, I don't have my reading glasses on."

I shrugged my shoulders, and with my hands held up suggesting *I give up* I walked away.
I wanted to say:
Well next time maybe you should ask and *what part of broken leg do you not get?* But I chose not to.

That same day as I was about to leave I said goodbye to Mia and headed towards the car park. As I looked back, despite the cones being there blocking the way, someone who was walking by with their horse stopped and let it put its head inside Mia's stable to apparently say hello.
I thought *really? This is just getting ridiculous!*
It simply was not ideal and as I was just about to walk back and say something, the very same person who had questioned me

earlier stepped over towards Mia's box and scolded them. I was astonished, they looked across at me now with a pitiful and understanding glance, and as they proceeded to drill the unsuspecting person with their new information I continued to walk away and could not help but have a small but celebratory skip in my stride.

This is one example of many questions and tireless escapades we endured. It was not all bad though, far from it in fact. We had many well wishes and support from those that cared and loved us, and we made many new friends. Such sweet gestures like buying Mia gifts, and chocolate or the odd bottle of wine for me, were continuous throughout those three months. With open arms we accepted the offering of things like reiki, healing touch and red light therapy. I first heard about and discovered the valuable use of red light therapy through my mentors on campus in the United States in 2010, and am adamant this aided in her recovery too, not just for its assistance in rebuilding cells and healing the body but also for general wellness and a good mind. Every single piece of help aided not just in getting Mia better, but also helped me conquer my inner battle of learning to live with the lack of control I had over her environment. The helplessness I felt when being cornered by other people, sometimes their cruelty or lack of integrity just floored me. I was too weak to fight and too kind to say no. As a working professional with some sort of reputation to uphold I could not very well go around and say what I really wanted to say, especially since my horses were boarded on somebody else's property.

In the end it was because of this particular confronting conversation that I decided to seriously search for another place for her to live directly after the x-ray, and to help make the rest of her recovery a success, if we ever got that far. In the Netherlands there are many rehabilitation centres for horses, two of which had been recommended by friends and which I had arranged to visit first. I was prepared to take her wherever the best place would be, even if it meant travelling with her to Germany or across the sea to England.

The first place I visited the guy had actually forgotten I was coming, not a good start and it meant nobody was there to show me around. I decided to do that myself and came to the fast conclusion the place was not for us. It was located next to a highway where you could feel the breeze of the cars as they passed. Although the place was kept clean and sterile, the horses really had nothing to look at except each other or a wall. It was just row upon row of stables and sad and sick looking horses. I think I was there ten minutes and I left feeling rather blue, not because I had not found her place yet, but because of the way the place made me feel. I hit the highway again a further two hours north to visit the second location. In the car I had this feeling of reluctance and a nagging thought told me to just turn around the car and head home, it was hard work to convince myself otherwise and keep driving. About halfway I almost lost control of my car as a huge stone hit my window and left a great big whopper of a crack in the windscreen. With my ears still ringing from the noise of the bang I pulled into a nearby gas station to access the damage. Fortunately it was the passenger's side and only one of the cracks had started to spread its way along towards the driver's side. It was a sign, that is what I told myself anyway, I should have turned back when I thought it earlier, but I was so close now a quick look would not hurt.

I soon forgot about the incident as I drove the rest of the way and as I arrived I was greeted by a middle aged man floating around on a Segway. He directed me to a parking place and gave me directions as to where to meet him, through a big green gate. I parked my car, gathered my thoughts and things and headed through the main entrance. It was a beautiful place, compared to the last one anyway. He gave me a grand tour of the location via an electric golf cart and as we drove around to view the property I started to realise the size of it, the place was huge. The choice available was nothing short of amazing, a five star hotel for horses. The stables ranged from anything from three metre by three meter, up to ten metre by ten metre. You could choose what type of hay you wanted to feed your horse and how many times a day *and* night. Some of the stables also had air conditioning, and it was after seeing that I realised it was going to be way out of my league. Perfect perhaps for those with a generous bank balance, but definitely not for little me.

After showing me the beautiful indoor arena, which by the way had mirrors all the way around on four walls, the hot water shower and massage area, the swimming pool and all the other luxury commodities, I started to get nervous to ask about the cost. After the tour he offered me a coffee on their beautiful terrace and proceeded to ask me what was wrong with my horse, what I thought of the property and what kind of care I needed if she were to come. He then presented me with a brochure with everything they had to offer, including the pricing. Relieved at not having to ask I carried on answering his questions, putting on my best poker face as my eyes glazed over the generous numbers. To be honest it was so expensive it would have been cheaper to mortgage my own farm. The minimum service of a three by three metre stable cleaned twice a day, with hay fed three times a during the day and one time at night, plus one meal per day for vitamins and supplements cost the same as my current mortgage. The cost for the largest stable with air conditioning alone and no extra services cost the same as my current mortgage and then some. Being a businessman of course he read my body language instantly and tried to convince me in so many words that if she was to stay longer than one year they could negotiate a lower price. Thanking him for his gesture I informed him I would think about it and get back to him in a few days. He left me to drink my second coffee and went about his business whilst I sat there contemplating the: *if only* in my head.

It was indeed a wonderful place, the horses were calm and I could hear birds singing in the many trees scattered across the acreage. As I got up to leave I saw him fly by on his Segway again, there were four horses with their heads hanging over the door of their stables snoozing in the late afternoon sun and as he passed each horse he reached for their heads to pull of the leather halters which had been left on, I can only assume as part of their daily routine or something like that. As he reached for the last horse it spooked, and regrettably he insisted the halter had to come off that way and there and then, resulting in the horse pulling backwards and hitting his nose on the top of the door. If I had all the money in the world, I was now certain I would not keep my beautiful horse there. One wrong push, pull or turn from this guy and I could only imagine what Mia's reaction would have been, and what scared me the most is what his reaction would have been in return. Besides all of that, we had already experienced what the top of a door could do to her nose.

A bit lost in my efforts, I did look at some other places and in my search figured out something that was bothering me. Against the veterinarian's recommendations I proceeded to think about the idea of having her in a quiet place where she could maybe stand in a small paddock, instead of the confines of four walls in a stable. I reached out to a possible contact, the same guy and Professional who had taught me during my first clinic with Mia, and who in due course had become a good friend. I sent him an email explaining the situation and that all I needed was a small paddock and her general needs taken care of, for a fee of course. He wrote back almost immediately telling me that he would love to help, and asked when I would bring her! I danced with happiness and joy as I typed my response and wrote back that she would have her x-ray on the 29th of August, and if all was well we would bring her there straight away that same afternoon. I was so incredibly grateful and relieved that we had a solution, now all we had to do was get through those last weeks and find out what the x-rays had to say.

On the 28th of August, we had a small send-off party with drinks and chairs outside her stable to celebrate her survival so far, and to wish her luck with the results of the x-rays the next day and with her future home. The girls had arranged a beautiful cake with her photo delicately situated on top, made out of sugar icing. It was a cosy but peculiar evening, knowing that the very next day things could go either way. Nobody had seen her walk for nearly three whole months, the thought still made me feel sick to the stomach but I continued to do my best and not show that in front of her. Anyhow, it did not matter, I should have known it there and then. Her energy, high spirit and willingness to socialise, be touched and loved by so many different people those past months already foretold the outcome: if there was anybody who knew that she was going to be okay, it was her.

CHAPTER 7

The road to recovery   The stuff dreams are made of

The big day arrived, after three months of seeing her unable to move and now expecting her to walk out of her stable directly into my trailer, it did send some butterflies through my stomach. My parents had flown over for support and together with a friend and my husband, we got ready for what I expected to be a very long trip. I had no idea how she would react with her first steps of freedom, however she walked out of the stable and into the trailer, which I had parked as close to her stable as possible, as though she had done it only the day before. What was even more remarkable was the way she walked, not only was she walking straight, she was bearing weight on the broken limb. Inside my heart skipped a thousand beats, on the outside I showed nothing, it was too good to be true. Scared of getting over excited, I also said nothing.

We arrived at the veterinary practice in no time where the head vet and his nurse were waiting to receive us. Still a man of few words, he did at least show some excitement and curiosity in his greeting. With unspoken communication he invited me to put her in the stock and left me alone to do so. Once again she entered the dark room and its hospital smell with those sceptical eyes, but step by step she trusted me to place her sideways into the stock. It was evident she was afraid, but for once I had a feeling that maybe she knew it was *for* her and not *to* her. All except of course the needle required for the sedation. She knew how and when that was going to happen and with some protest of course we managed to inject her. The routine we had adapted, although a predictable move to Mia, was all I could do in an effort to restrain her violent reaction towards the vet, and his deathly needle. I set the rope in such a way that if she was quiet and calm the rope would stay loose, and if she went to bite him the rope tightened itself. She released herself very quickly after feeling that and in less than ten seconds it was over. My parents and husband stayed outside, and my friend and I stayed inside for the effects of the drug to kick in. There she was again slowly slipping into a tranquilised state, so beautiful, so strong and so very innocent.

Ten minutes later the vet and his assistant re-entered the room and my friend left while we put on the lead aprons and they prepared the x-ray machine. I stood with Mia at her head again, watching this strange machine move around the room like a giant noisy snake, and once it was in position she started to stir. I shared a glance with the vet where he gave me that reassuring look, except this time we both knew what could happen. As the assistant set about placing the x-ray plate between her legs he started to sing again and *click* it was done, followed by a hasty but smooth adjustment of the machine for a front angle and *click* it was done again. Mia, the assistant and I gave a huge sigh of relief and the vet made his way to his little side room to study the x-rays.

It was at this point something inside me truthfully knew she was going to be okay, I still dared not say it out loud but the way she had walked backwards off the trailer and the way she walked into the building, how could it not be? My friend came back into the room and helped me wait through the agonising moments of not knowing what would happen next. Finally the moment had arrived and he called me into his room with a warm but cautious smile. Before he spoke, my eyes scanned the computer screens, looking and searching for any difference. He started to explain that the bone had indeed begun to heal the way it should and had started to form a bony callous connecting the broken piece to the parent bone. Apart from the day I got married and a few other memorable life occasions, I cannot recall ever having been so happy. The atmosphere in the room changed from gloomy anticipation to bright celebration.

However I was quickly reminded that we were not out of the woods yet, there was still a long way to go. The bone had to continue healing the way it was or it could put the quality of her life, or her actual life, at risk. I thanked the vet more than necessary and set about putting Mia back in the trailer to head to her new home. I made an agreement with him to bring her back in about one year to re-examine the leg, sooner if I had any concerns. In parting he wished us all the best for the foreseeable future.

We arrived just a minute short of five hours, a journey which should have only taken us three but was delayed because of local traffic. As we entered the premises I could finally feel my shoulders and body relax. I don't think they had really relaxed that much since before she was diagnosed with the broken leg. I have never been a fan of trailering horses at the best of times, especially sick ones, it is not the trailer or the road I am afraid of, it is other drivers and their impatience. The types of roads in the Netherlands can be exceptionally narrow, only irritating drivers more if they cannot pass.

It was so great to be there and with a huge welcome from my friends I unloaded Mia and placed her in her new paddock. It was so much nicer than I had ever expected, it could not have been more suitable for our situation and my wishes. The paddock area was set up inside an old but cosy barn, some forty feet long and twenty feet wide. The paddock dominated one corner with six foot high aluminium panelling especially designed for horses. Next to it were two large stables and the feed storage. In the middle was a corridor wide enough for a tractor to pass through, on the opposite far end was a hay storage area and directly across from her lived her new friends, something she had never really seen before, and that was the donkeys.

The paddock had a hard dry concrete floor to encourage her to walk slowly and move around a little without tripping over or slipping, and in the corner was some fresh straw which she could do with what she liked. There was a huge water bucket and a slow feeding hay-net filled with beautiful fresh smelling hay.

Coming off the trailer she knew where she was, having previously spent around six weeks in total at the same place for various clinics and study days, so it did not take her long to settle down and relax. She immediately tucked into the hay and occasionally investigated the space; that is until her new donkey neighbours appeared. They too had a similar set up on the opposite side, the only difference being that it was of course much bigger and they could roam free outside into a large paddock. It was quite comical to see the little guys come over and inquisitively watch their new neighbour: a big black horse who had momentarily become afraid, but also very curious. Although donkeys look like horses and are from the same family, they do move and smell differently and some horses can have quite some trouble being confident when they are around. Mia evidently had a small shock but soon grew to fall in love with them. It took a few feeding times where the donkeys made a lot of noise called braying instead of neighing, for her to really get used to them. The noise would echo around the barn and I can imagine with a low wind the noise could travel some miles too. With all of that and the possibility for her to move around, it did not bother me like it had in the stable back home. She had already proven to us all in so many ways that given the time and a chance to figure things out she could take care of herself, I trusted that, I owed her that much. Another benefit was not having to give her an oral sedative anymore, this was much better for her health overall and sat more in line with my own principles and philosophy.

Not long after dropping her off we left to return home, I had made arrangements to leave my trailer there and visit the following weekend. A new beginning had begun; she was now able to rest in the peace and quiet of this idyllic location and was cared for by people I loved and trusted beyond words.

I visited her as much as I could, usually something like once every four to six weeks. To be honest their kindness made it easy for me to do that, so it did not matter if I could not come sooner at times. Those initial days were strange without her around, having been there for her every single one of those painful days, battling to protect her and make her feel safe, when I suddenly did not have to anymore it left an impermanent gaping hole in my daily schedule. Distance does indeed make the heart grow fonder and every time during the last few kilometres of my journey on my way to visit her I would find myself humming or smiling at the thought of seeing her shortly. That winter was pretty hard, with snowfall and lots of hard rain. The place where her paddock was situated could not be more perfect, allowing protection against the wind and rain in the winter and cool shade in the summer. She grew fond of her donkeys, not afraid anymore they helped create an ambient environment. Donkeys carry an almost therapeutic quality about them, and I am sure Mia benefited from that. In the summer and dry months they would come out of their paddock area and walk across the barn to a pasture close by, and Mia would always welcome them back with a motherly whinny and some form of happiness with a small skip and head shake. As the months passed we made many more new friends, and one lady in particular took it upon herself to take Mia under her wing by giving her extra care. She did things like brushing and cleaning her hooves and put toys in her water. She also sat with her and placed edible trees in the paddock to give her something to do, and to chew on. Sometimes she would have the children help her, and as far as I can tell Mia enjoyed the attention. I named her Mia's guardian angel, and just like my friends who made the quick yet effortless decision to help us and take her on, I don't think I will ever be able to extend my gratitude and thanks enough.

By the spring of 2014 Mia appeared to be doing incredibly well. Although certain things were obvious, for example having lost most of her muscle mass, and her hooves although trimmed on a regular basis took quite their toll, she showed us she was doing just fine in her good spirit and energy.
To function correctly a horse's hooves can be thought of as four additional hearts, every step that they take enables blood to circulate inside them to keep the wall of the hoof and its internal

structure healthy. Of course not being able to move further than the limits of her luxury paddock, their formation did change. A small sacrifice, if you consider the horse was still alive and standing there in front of all of our proud selves. In an effort to help her with that, and give her a new quality of life we opened the paddock behind her. Being the same in size as the existing paddock, it gave her a new space to explore and move around, and with the added bonus of old sand and compost covering the ground she could also roll to her heart's content. Despite humanity's efforts to keep these majestic and wilful animals clean, they really do love to be dirty. Like most mammals it does wonders for their skin and hair, helps to keep bugs and skin infections at bay and allows the horse to stretch its body and back in a way they cannot whilst standing up. The paddock also gave her a new view of the barn where she could watch her beloved donkeys on their pasture, and she could stand for a few hours in the passing sun. In reflection I have nothing but admiration for this horse, she did it by herself. With unknown communication and energy she resigned to the idea that she was going to be there for a long time, and without pain relief or the help of drugs to keep her calm, she did just that.

With Mia on the road to recovery I delved into my work at a deeper level. I gave Kheelen as much time as a young horse could handle, and as for the rest of life, it went on relatively normally. However, the universe presented me with another challenge, something that had been tucked away deep inside my ignorance to carry on with life and just get on with it, and that was another burnout. Unless it is understood or one has experienced this feeling themselves, it is very hard to explain. What I do know is that sometimes people like myself have no other way to cope, and rather than let your feelings take their natural course in one go at the time of an event or change in life, we tend to bottle it all up instead. For me the feelings had already exposed themselves at the time when Kheelen was sick, and through the period Mia had the hoof abscess right up to the time I found out her leg was broken. Somewhere, somehow I had managed to put it all away, but over the winter of 2013 into 2014 it finally took hold of my very being and body taking all of my confidence with it, and I defaulted to what I thought was my weaker self. I became extremely introverted and fell back to that place where I stopped believing in myself. I gained almost twelve kilos that winter and come the following spring was very conscious of it. Doing the type of work I do with people and horses requires you to be fairly physical, always active and constantly on your feet, so in my mind the weight gain was incredibly unfair if you also consider my diet had not changed either. An unhealthy or negative mind can quickly create an unhealthy or negative response in a body, and upon this realisation I was diagnosed with a not just a burnout but also a mild but serious enough form of depression. To hear somebody tell you that, and to tell you personally that the reason you feel like shit is because you are depressed is quite something to take on, and if you are not careful it can bring you down even harder. With professional help I learned to embrace it and see it as a positive reason to get back on my feet, fight the weight and carry on. The most important lesson I learned from all of it was that it was not a weakness, it was a strength to be able to hold on to all of my emotions like that and to not let them go. It takes a strong person to do that and sometimes when the body cannot hold on anymore it has to find a way to let go, this was my body's way of saying *let go*!

In hindsight I can think of periods in my life where without knowing it, I had maybe been suffering from some form of depression. I gained a few kilos sometimes but nothing of this magnitude, and all it took was a change in lifestyle, routine or a positive life event to help it blow over. Behind the scenes I worked incredibly hard to feel well again, no easy task when everything is an effort and all you want to do is snuggle up on the sofa and disappear into a movie or the land of sleep, yet somehow I did it. I lost some friends along the way who did not understand the situation as well as some who did not want to, and that is okay, it is what it is, I am who I am and they are who they are. I have grown so much and have learned to understand

145

the human body and mind probably more than most. In return I can help people in my teachings with their personal lives, and help their horses do the same.

In June of 2014 although still not at my best, I made a trip to the USA for six weeks to study and teach on campus and further my education, it was perfect timing. Mia was still away and Kheelen was still so young that a holiday for him raised no objections. Whilst in America I stayed in touch with Mia's carers and they sent me the most amazing footage of Mia standing in their private lake playing with the water. We had decided to judge it on feeling as far as she was concerned, and they had started to take her for small walks around the property for ten minutes or so to give her another new quality of life. It got to the point where in the last two weeks she was there she was set loose to be free for a few hours a day in a small pasture; for the first time in a long time she could eat grass and start to be a horse again. I actually thought that in all fairness she would never be rideable again anyway so it could not hurt. The knowledge that she was happy to live this way again and had the best care in the world, it all aided my recovery and when I got home from my trip the kilos finally started to subside. After many thanks and gratitude I could finally take Mia home, as her guardian angel had said:
"It was time."

CHAPTER 8

Black noise   The second fracture, wonderment

Mia as ever, will call out when we are on the road which leads to her home, and as usual all the way along the tree canopied street and right up to where you enter the premises, I could feel the trailer move in her excitement. A moment that made me confident that we were doing all the right things, she was alive and she was letting everyone know that. She spent the night in a paddock with Kheelen and the next day we headed to the vets for her check-up and x-ray. With a friend we drove the short distance deep in conversation about what my plans might be next. Arriving early we had to wait a while, so I unloaded Mia and walked her around the property to have a browse and eat some grass; this was something we had not had the opportunity to do before. As she walked I could not help but notice her stumble once or twice on her right front leg, I quickly convinced myself it was nothing to worry about and that maybe it was just her hooves being over sensitive after all of that time resting.

The vet greeted me with the same smile and anticipation he had the year before, and this time before inviting me to put her in the stock he asked to see her move around a bit first. We entered a round pen with a hard concrete surface where he could observe her moving on a circle both left and right in walk and then in trot. To my horror she was lame, to a certain extent we could celebrate because the broken hind leg was moving the way it should and showed no sign of trouble, it was her front right leg that now captured our attention. He asked to see her move once more on a straight line, where it was still there but less obvious, and then he asked politely with some doubtful humour if he could physically try to examine her.

Something inside me did not hesitate and with a supporting smile I gestured for him to proceed. Not only did she let him touch her, she let him pick up her new painful leg to examine it and did so without as much as a flinch of resistance. It took me a few moments to realise what was happening, and to my delight even despite the unwelcome situation we had found ourselves in, if we were to look at it from the point of view of the past, it was a memorable moment. After some poking and prodding to try and find out where there could be pain, his suggestion was to do what is called a nerve block, where you inject a local anaesthetic like a dentist would to numb your gums and in doing so help eliminate and determine where the lameness is coming from: a common practice used for many years in the horse industry for diagnostic purposes.

She allowed him to inject her foot, and acting the way she does with me and her guardians she even offered to hold up her leg to help. For the last fourteen years, all of the worrying, battling, giving excuses and having to explain our problem to people and most importantly her attending doctors, in my eyes this was nothing short of astonishing. He too in fact had to smile and made a joke that maybe the time away had somehow fixed her. It was a nice moment, yet short lived when the nerve block revealed nothing and we decided it was best to just x-ray her front leg too. Going through the same process as before, entering the examination room and moving sideways into the stock followed by a tranquiliser was nothing new to her now, and I was relieved to see that despite probably not having the best memories in that room she did not appear to question it.

He called me into his side room and showed me the left hind knee x-rays first. The fracture had continued to heal and connect well and in comparison to the last picture even my untrained eye could see the difference.

His only warning was that the callous bone growth which had formed was most likely weak and there was no way to judge that, so it was not possible to determine whether it would break again. Those last words were soon brushed aside in my thoughts as he diverted my attention to the results of the next x-rays from her right front hoof. In his tone I could tell he could not quite believe what he had to tell me, which was that she had indeed broken another bone. The first time those words left his mouth over a year before, I fell into a deep state of unconscious incompetence which I refer to as *White noise*. This time I fell into an unconscious competence which I refer to as *Black noise*. I managed to ask him questions like how and why this could have happened, and not quite believing it I felt some anger inside. Not at him and of course not at Mia, but at the universe challenging us yet again.

As I saw Mia standing there not knowing what in the world was happening I felt so much sadness for her. This poor beautiful horse who had come so far. It was as if a black veil had been pulled over my heart, yet somehow I found the strength inside me to fight for us again, I had to do it for her. By using the powers I had used to heal myself and the new person I had started to become, I knew I was not about to stop now, and logically I began to pick up the pieces of how to fix this next challenge.

It was of some relief to hear that the fracture this time was something the vet had seen before, unfortunately on too many occasions. It is a common injury found in horses with careers like show jumping and it can happen when the hoof bears too much weight all at once or too often, over an extensive amount of time.

She had what is called a wing fracture of the coffin bone, and in comparison to the human anatomy the coffin bone is equivalent to the bone that sits under our fingernail. Horses walk on their fingertips so to speak. The coffin bone sits fully within the hoof capsule and is suspended off of the ground by the rest of the structure of the hoof called Laminae. It was a significant injury, and such fractures cause instability with each and every step the horse takes.

149

It is funny how things work, the very essence of my education so far and what I had been teaching to other people and their horses could not have been given a better example. In order to climb, one must fall first, the higher the climb the harder the fall and when one eventually reaches the top, the reward is plentiful. We had not climbed quite high enough yet, but what I had acknowledged and to this day do my very best to maintain, was the change in myself and how it influenced my horse. Recuperation from the depression had evolved me into a new person with a new attitude and a new confidence. I would not go as far as saying I was reborn, but reawakened perhaps, and Mia knew this. When the vet examined her, a thought that she might have a problem with that had not entered my mind. When he presented the needle which he had to inject into her painful foot she did not react, nor did I. My horse had given me another life lesson and having been told by my mentors a thousand times I had now experienced it first hand, and knew exactly what they were talking about, and I mean *really* talking about. They say match your horse's energy and not their emotions, meaning the problem she had with the needles stemmed half from what I thought about it and half from what she thought about it. My thoughts were projected in my body language, and no matter how minimal it was she saw it, let us not forget that horses are masters of reading body language.

I was still at the beginning of understanding these things then as I still am today, and I am only honest when I say if any one person tries to tell you differently or claim that they know it all they are most certainly a liar, simply because there is so much to learn. In the years before we moved to the Netherlands, right up to the point where I wanted to sell her I thought that we did not have a bond. The idea in my mind was something like one's horse galloping across the pasture to see you when you called them, I was very wrong and indeed narrow minded. She taught me to open my mind and see the endless possibilities of what a bond can look and feel like. Mia might not gallop across the pasture and follow me around like my dreams told me they should, what she does do is share her inner emotions and her

150

own personal way of apportioning time. She has a time with no clock, looking towards me for some sort of leadership, proven because my negative thoughts and emotions do influence hers. Kheelen on the other hand does come running when I call him, he reflects more the ideal picture that I had and which millions of people still do have around the globe today. The difference is, they are all individuals just like you and I; no two horses are alike. During my battles with depression, one of the things I struggled with the most was that I did not like myself, I felt angry a lot of the time and for reasons I cannot even remember I convinced myself I was a bad person. Although I did not mean any of it I could not control it, I also struggled to understand why somebody like me who had everything they ever wanted could feel this way, and it was something that my husband said once again one day that got me really thinking, he said:

"You are not a bad person, how can you think you are a bad person, just take a look at your animals!"

What wise words, if I were truly a mean or bad person, the first place you would have seen it would have been in the animals surrounding my life. My past struggles with Mia reflected this, which is true; however it was not related in terms of my abusing her or my being mean to her, it was more to do with who I was in terms of confidence. She was and still is a sweet and kind horse as I have always been to her. On particularly difficult days when for example I have to handle people who do not agree, understand or do not want to know why I do the things I do and go out of their way to make my life more challenging, I know I can rely on one thing and that is them. The animals lift me up and build a bridge I can walk or run over and one that I do not have to look back across if I do not want to; it gives me incredible strength and self-value.

If we are to talk about my golden boy Kheelen, he is a bundle of light, his energy and spirit shines on every single day. He is cheeky, funny and an absolute pleasure; he is the best of me all in one package. Almost every day at least one person will comment how happy my little dog is or they are surprised at how happy she is towards them. Even on my darkest days, she would selflessly take care of me and find a way to make me smile. Then there is Mia, my lioness; she mirrors my feelings towards people and places, she is the best and the worst of me and everything that is right or indeed wrong about me and I know one thing for sure, she is perfect.

CHAPTER 9   Part I

You *will* be lucky again   Great expectations

This road to recovery was with some relief far less tricky than the first one, and the veterinarian's parting words were:

"You will be lucky again."

This was music to my ears since we now had another three to four months of rest ahead of us, and I still had to arrange it at the barn. The plan was straightforward enough; his recommendation had been to find a blacksmith also known as a farrier as soon as possible, who could make two iron shoes. One of them would need to be specially shaped to fix the broken hoof, and the healthy hoof could wear a regular and traditional iron shoe for balance and to aid in the compensation of the broken hoof. The most common and customary shape of an iron horseshoe is a ring shape of which one fifth or thereabouts is missing, creating a gap. The gap is fitted at the back of the horse's hoof facing towards the heel, and during the making of the shoe they usually add a clip or a lip to hold the shoe in place at the toe and opposite the heel, not all shoes have a lip but the majority do. The shoe that the vet wanted the blacksmith to create for the broken hoof would have at least five lips to protect the circumference of the hoof wall, and act like some sort of brace or cast. Thankfully he said it with such confidence it was obvious this was not new to him, and that it would probably not be a new request to an experienced blacksmith either. He was also pleasantly optimistic that with the correct shoe and given time to rest it would heal. However he did say that the shoe had to fit perfectly, and he advised me that once I found a blacksmith I was to ask them to call him and he would help explain his request and the situation. Phew!

It was a huge consolation that the barn manger agreed she could live this time in a sand paddock located on the other side of the barn next to where some other horses were already living too. This was a wonderful gesture, and although the paddock was a bit bigger in size than the vet had suggested I could not turn it down, and without the space to run around too much and the company of other horses she found it easy to relax and settled almost immediately. I asked around for help to find a reputable blacksmith urgently, one of the girls found one and even offered to make the call and reference him to the vet, it was all arranged so quickly. The blacksmith came the next day, made the shoes and fitted them exactly to the vet's requirements. I was advised that she was to wear the shoes for six weeks and then replace them with new ones again.

For the next appointment I had arranged to meet the blacksmith at the vet practice to remove the shoes there, view the x-rays and replace and make the new shoes again. We did just that and the vet was pleased to inform us the fracture was indeed healing and that we were to just keep doing what we were doing for at least the next two months. It was amazing to observe such a huge fracture that had dominated one side of her hoof almost disappear and so quickly. Due to time and a clash of schedules I could not arrange for the blacksmith to meet me there that time, but had arranged for him to meet me at the barn later that same day. So the vet removed the shoes himself and in doing so admired the iron work. It really was quite something. He also advised me that we could reduce the lips to three instead of five to start allowing her foot some movement and room to rehabilitate itself. It was a time to celebrate and I could not wait to share the news with my husband, family and friends.

I had gone to great lengths after moving to The Netherlands to remove Mia's iron horse shoes and learn to live without them, it was not only possible because of the way the horses lived on a mix of soft and hard ground but also because of a balanced diet, good exercise and regular trimming by a professional in that trade. The blacksmith was my kind of guy, although his trade and knowledge was specifically about shoeing horses, he was also very open to not wearing them too and I am truly grateful for that. Today there is so much information available, telling you why horses wearing shoes is both a good thing and a bad thing; it would be difficult not to question your own decisions. My advice to anyone wanting to make a change or do things differently is to simply do plenty of research first in your immediate environment, and not on a website located on the other side of the globe. Go out of your way to find out all of the how and not just the why. It is not always ideal having a professional from overseas telling you that what they do is best when they have control over the environment of the horse, or the environment of their horse is completely different. With that I mean food, exercise, climate, footing etc.

What I advise anyone to do is to take on board as much information as possible and to then do their best to adapt it to their environment, or to follow the lead of a good example of someone that already does what they would like to do. It is also important not to take too much advice from too many people, only from a select few and again people who are a good example. I personally would not take advice from someone who perhaps has problems with their horse's hooves, I just would not. I would look only perhaps at the people who had problems that got better, or had no issues at all. That is exactly what I did in this situation; I was not necessarily happy about Mia wearing the iron shoes, but I was willing to do it because somebody I respected had proven to me already so far that he only had her best interests at heart, and was a good enough example for me to follow.

So, how did Mia break her hoof?
A question I hear often of course. The conclusion we came up with, and one that again I have learned to live with in an effort to remove the, *what if?* And the *If only,* is:

155

It is possible that such a big horse, having learned to live with the left hind broken leg had over compensated her weight and movement on the right foreleg. The break may have started small and could have grown in size over a period of time. As surprised as we were at this second incident, it seemed logical, and since people do not usually give their horses a chance like I had or are not always as fortunate as I had been to let her heal in such a suitable environment for such a long time, we had nothing to compare it to. I can be sure of one thing, that Mia knew all along that something was wrong. Along with several witnesses I watched her learn how to cope with the broken hind leg and give herself the time that she needed to heal, without medicine or additional medical help. Over the period of the first fracture and the second fracture she was fed good quality hay and a vitamin supplement which carried a higher than average dose of things like magnesium, zinc and sulphur, all of which aid in bone and tissue growth.

However what must not be forgotten is that this horse was given time; time to rest, time to heal and time to recover, and eventually in a suitable and positive environment. I am aware this is a luxury not within everybody's reach, but with things like today's social media and the ability to reach out beyond the walls of our homes, it is very possible to put the feelers out and maybe find a place like I did which can offer a sick horse a positive place to heal. I am not referencing or advising that all injuries and broken bones can be healed this way, but it should get us thinking that many things are possible and if somebody were to fail after trying, at least they did try. We can all learn from results like that and help evolve modern medicine and treatment programs not just for horses, but for other large animals too. That is the main reason why I wanted to share this story.

CHAPTER 9   Part II

They call it a miracle   Because it was

Miracle: a remarkable event or development that brings very welcome consequences, or a person or thing that is a marvellous example of something.

By 2014 the word of Mia's broken bones and her recovery was quite something, having reached the eyes and ears of hundreds, maybe thousands of people, and was constantly the highlight of most of my conversations. Although dampened a little by time since the events took place, I often find myself talking proudly about it today.

Since she was healing so well and so fast with the three lipped shoe, the vet advised me to keep them on as long as possible. The rest of that winter would be ideal, exchanging them every six to eight weeks for new ones. We did this, and after four months I was finally allowed to start her rehabilitation program. During the second month of her rest I had already introduced her into a different but small paddock to keep another recovering horse company. As of today they are still the best of friends. Mia was not showing any signs of lameness anywhere, and the most rewarding part was being able to give her contact with another horse again, it went perfectly. Winter arrived quickly and with a very wet summer behind us and the air turning cooler each day, the horses were brought in off of the land to the paddocks for the next six months, a week earlier than usual. Therefore I had to make some on the spot decisions by either finding another home for her again or reintroducing her back into her old herd, something that had to happen eventually anyway. I considered all the odds and like any decision I had to make from that moment forward, it carried a big risk. It was here I decided to put her back with her herd. Naturally it worried me and gave me quite a few sleepless nights, and although the paddock's size was not questionable it was the ground and footing that worried me, consisting half of a sandy area and half of hard concrete area. Horses that wear iron shoes on concrete or tarmac can slip and slide very easy. Mia being her big, powerful alpha self did not fair too badly.

As the winter passed and the New Year arrived I started to introduce her to a strict regime of planned exercise, therapeutic massages and osteopath treatments. Her first introduction to a work regime had started with a ten minute walk in hand each day on hard ground for a week, then twice a day for a week. Followed by ten minutes' walk on hard ground and ten minutes' walk on soft ground, then followed by five minutes of trot added to that once a day, then twice a day and so forth. The first time I sat on her and rode her again was amazing, the feelings I had were more than I can articulate. It was captured on film by one of my students and is a day I shall never forget.
Riding her helped a great deal since she had to learn how to carry weight on the healed joints again and I could start to help her use her body better, something which I could not judge or feel as well on the ground as I could from her back. Replacing some of her ground work, the riding was also built up from ten minutes' walk, to ten minutes' walk plus five minutes of trot until we got to the point where things were almost normal again. When she was ready I also took her on a few trail rides in the dunes and introduced cavalletti, which means placing poles on the ground situated perfectly for the horse to step over, helping them to lift their legs aiding in gymnastic ability and suppleness. Although I am not a bad rider, I am not one of the best ones either, but I do work hard at it and since Mia was so out of shape, had muscle atrophy in many different places and formed evidentially a bad posture too, it was in my best interest to really start to understand and master the art of dressage again and use it to help her get back on her feet. She was and still can be today if you let her, a very heavy horse on the forehand, meaning she will put more

weight on her front legs and not carry herself behind, she would rather push herself along than carry herself. By riding her I could help her with this and re-teach her not only how to use her body again, but also how to lift her shoulders, carry weight on the hind legs and dare I say it, do it better than she ever did before. Naturally I had conversations with the vet with regards to what we could and could not do, probably for the rest of her life. The limits we agreed on were more than fair. Jumping was one of them and even the odd jump here or there was simply out of the question and too much of a risk; a shame since she always showed great enthusiasm jumping obstacles or barrels and the bigger the better. Trail rides longer than three hours were also out of the question, the last thing was allowing her to run at full speed in gallop with a rider on board for too long, and by too long meaning maybe getting up to that speed but dropping back down to the lower speed of canter again as soon as possible.

Not a bad deal, still here and able to live a relatively normal life, one cannot argue with that. I also decided to just let the horse show me what she could and could not do, and whilst working with her I would also figure things out along the way. I was so incredibly happy and proud to be making these decisions and plans. At one time I would never have thought it all possible, thinking if she did get through it she would end up being a very welcome pet. To have her as my partner and a riding companion once again was simply phenomenal, and a cause for many celebrations. They call it a miracle simply because it was, it is a miracle that the bone grew back and reattached because it had an upward force exerted on it with every step she made. It is a miracle that she recovered and it is a miracle that she wanted to recover. Personally I like to think of miracles happening not because we wait for them to happen, but because we make them happen. Mia made it happen.

CHAPTER 9   Part III

That dreaded call   <small>The universe calling again</small>

Not long before full spring had arrived and just prior to another
appointment for her new shoes, I pondered on the idea of
whether to cancel the lifesaving skills of the blacksmith and
replace it with my regular barefoot trimmer again. It felt like it
was time, and during the last appointment I had a briefing with
the head vet and he had recommended we reduce the lips on the
special shoe down to one so she was actually for that time just
wearing two regular iron shoes on both hooves.
The paddocks are located in the middle of the barn grounds and
to reach the area where my equipment is stored you have to walk
past them. In doing so you can observe the horses, and on an
average day depending on my schedule I might do that anything
between ten and twenty times. Because of my interest, profession
and love for horses you will often find me standing either inside
the paddock to watch them or outside, perhaps while eating my
lunch learning and observing their behaviour. Other times just
for fun I will go and stand with my own horses and watch them
eat or simply hang out. That winter so far I had seen many things
in Mia I had not seen before, and as the months passed it became
apparent it was not going to change. In the past when entering
the paddock or a pasture it did not matter how many horses stood
in your way, as soon as her energy was present they would move
out of her way. You would often hear me joke around saying
something like:

"They part like the red sea did for Moses when Mia is around."

This amazing presence is a part of who she is, and I also think it
was something that played a huge part in why she is still here

today. I would not say she was at the bottom of the pecking order, but she was certainly not at the crown adorning top either. In her then fifteen years of life, I had never seen her run away from other horses as much as I saw then. Two things itched and scratched at the back of my mind, the first was that maybe she felt weaker and was treated weaker now because of the previously broken bones, or the iron shoes made her feel less secure on her feet, I was hoping for the second conclusion. In the wild with a broken leg she would have been on the food chain and most likely would have died.

By the powers of Mother Nature and instinct she knew this and I am certain the other horses knew this too, yet I so badly hoped removing the shoes would be the resolution. I weighed up all of the pros and cons and finally decided to cancel the appointment with the blacksmith and take a risk by going barefoot again. There was an easy solution, if she was sore on her hooves or I thought something was not right I could simply change my mind and put the shoes back on. The vet had not given me a specific timeline, his only advice was to leave the shoes on as long as possible. For me this was as long as possible and I could not wait to take them off her. My barefoot hoof trimmer came and removed the shoes. Mia was exceptionally quiet, it was as if she somehow knew they would not be going back on. As I led her back to her paddock she did something I realised momentarily she had not done for a long time, she trotted next to me in anticipation to move forwards.

I questioned myself: *it had to be a good choice, how could it not be?*

Entering the paddock we proceeded with our ritual of her lowering her head and waiting for me to remove her halter, she did so with precise patience, a promise we both kept, and as I set her free she turned on her hind quarters and cantered across the paddock, she was free.

It was an unforgettable moment, the shoes had indeed been nothing more than a pain in the ass and she was restricted when wearing them. I am glad that I listened to my gut feeling, that maybe because of her weaker hind knee she had felt like she could not protect herself as well as she could without them. The display she gave pretty much confirmed all of that. A few days passed and she never became sore on her hooves. Forever thankful and a little sad I that would not see him again, I never made a new appointment with our steel shoe making hero.

That spring I had another decision to make, to either let her go out on the pasture again with the other horses for the summer, or to keep her on the paddock where she would be much safer; initially I decided she would stay on the paddocks. The day the horses were set free on the land I had to teach a clinic in another location, her new carer made sure she was kept busy as the change happened and set her back in the paddock once everything was settled. Thankful for this but feeling somewhat downhearted at my decision, I could not help but think how wonderful it would be to see her out in the fields of lush green grass with her herd mates again. The tug and pull of the last two and a half years was strong and fed my weaker side, so I gave out. When I returned, while walking my dog towards the dunes I saw the horses having a great time in the open green fields, I thought: *sod it, after all that she has been through, why not let her have her time?*

I fetched her from her paddock, walked her into the field and let her eat some grass before setting her free. Mia being Mia showed her old habits by walking ten or twelve feet and then bursting off into a full gallop. I could not help but smile, it was a beautiful display, she was free the best way a horse can be and she was incredibly happy.

Fair play to Mia, she held her ground proudly, she established her leadership quickly and for a few weeks did well on the grass. A bit too well actually, and it got to the point that she was fast becoming obese. The option of putting her in a diet pasture no longer existed and even if it was available I would not have had the courage to do that again, so I had to make a new decision for the sake of her health. It made sense, I could control her diet better anyway and if we continued this way her weight would be too heavy to carry on her weaker limbs, she had to come back to the paddocks. I had never seen her pissed off for so long before, for a whole week she ate very little, she stood by the gate closest to the pastures which she could not see, but could only hear the distant replies to her calls and quite literally waited in the hope that somebody, anybody would take her back. She was okay when I took her out of the paddock, but when I put her back her suggestion of going past the paddock gate entrance and towards the green grass was soft but relentless. I did pity her but had to do what was best for her health, you could say however and to some degree, she was temporarily depressed.

There were twelve maybe fifteen other horses living with her on the paddock and the hierarchy in the herd was not in order yet. Probably due to the fact that the horses knew the grass was indeed greener on the other side. Notably there were two mares causing quite a stir and using their best efforts to try and claim the crown. In my observation, seeing how nasty these girls could be to each other, they were working too hard and far too long for it. A wild horse, usually a stallion might spend days claiming such a position for breeding rights but in a domesticated horse I had not seen such a violent and relentless display go on for so long before. Once Mia had resigned to the fact that she would indeed not be heading back to the pastures and that the paddocks were indeed her place of safety and food, she finally started to pay attention and mingle with the herd again. She had apparently been almost invisible that week and once visible again she fought off one of the mares pretty quickly, a small battle of teeth and shaved hair and it was done. But the other mare was not so easy to convince and for a few weeks I would witness them fight in passing or would be working with a student nearby only to hear a horse battle erupt from the paddocks, it was mostly Mia and her opponent, they were incessant.

It was during a weekend where I was enjoying the luxury of a rare day off with my husband that I received *that dreaded call*.

163

A kind lady whom I also teach was at the barn and happened to witness an extra-long and violent fight between the two mares. Apparently Mia in her efforts to kick back lost her footing and her back legs gave out underneath her, the mare finished her off with one final kick to the ribs before walking off to get back to her business probably eating hay. I am not mad at the horse she fought with, it does not make sense to be mad, this is their language, this is the way horses communicate and Mia this day appeared to be the weaker party. She told me on the phone that Mia was incredibly lame, she could barely walk and that I was to come as soon as I could. I did not hang about, thankfully my husband drove me to the barn while I called the vet for an emergency visit.

As we arrived at the entrance and drove along the driveway of the barn I had a sudden rush of nausea thinking this was it, I was going to lose her. It was a shock to see her as I arrived, her stomach was tight just like it had been that day I found her on the pasture and her butt and lower right hind leg was covered from top to bottom in kick marks and welts, imprinted perfectly from the concrete where she had fallen. Upon further examination and trying to keep my cool it was obvious she could not walk, but this time equally to my horror it was not her left hind leg that was hurting it was her right hind leg. For the love of horses I could not believe it, there and then my thoughts were that maybe she had broken the right hind knee too.

The vet arrived minutes after we had, I was relieved and happy with her presence, a small girl in height and stature she approached us with a warm smile. Knowing Mia's story very well from her past visits to the practice, she proceeded to ask questions and then set about examining her. I can only admire the situation really, although it was absolutely not a position any of us wanted to be in, Mia surprisingly with all her extremities proved something to all of us once more. She not only accepted the girl's friendly greeting and touch, she also aided the vet in her examination by lifting the very painful leg. In order to compare the hind knees with each other to check for abnormalities and swelling she needed to stand directly behind Mia with her chest and body resting on her tail, whilst reaching forward with both arms. I, together with the small audience that had now gathered, shared an unspoken admiration not just for Mia but also for the vet in attendance. I was, for lack of better words gobsmacked. She confirmed there and then she did not think anything was broken, however there was a small amount of swelling on the right knee joint and that she certainly had some nasty bruises along her right quarters and down her leg. She advised that for peace of mind an additional solution if I wanted to, was to take a blood sample. They would send it immediately to the laboratory for analysis where in a day or two they could read the enzymes in the blood and tell if there was bone trauma, and the extent of any muscle damage. I was impressed, never having heard of this before and naturally I said yes. We also agreed that I would give her a minimum of five days oral pain relief and anti-inflammatory to aid in her recovery.

If the vet had for one moment predicted there was some kind of fracture she would not have advised to give pain relief for the very same reasons as the occasion before, simply because it is best if the horse knows there is something wrong in order to encourage them to rest. This all gave me great comfort, and in my bid to stay positive I saw a sparkling glint in Mia's eyes, it was as if she told me in that moment:

"Just a small set back, everything will be fine!"

Out of Mia's sight the vet prepared the needle and unconcerned she approached Mia, held the area where the arterial vein sits in a horse's neck to expose it and proceeded to take the blood. Mia simply stood there without so much as a flinch, as the larger than normal needle entered a life line and drew precious blood. The vet was equally impressed, not only did Mia accept the treatment, she snuffled and snuggled into her arms after the deed was done and by judging the smile on my face she knew it was a special time.

165

The attending vet's final advice was to allow her twenty four hours rest somewhere isolated from the herd until her leg felt better and she was more mobile again. Inside the paddock under the roof of a moderately sized barn that the horses use for shelter were two empty stables, which could now be used for sick and ailing horses. With the help of a friend whom by now was also taking care of Mia one day a week, we made a nice straw bed and put a generous amount of hay in the corner that she could munch. Upon taking her there it was evident she was already walking seventy five percent better than ten minutes prior, and it was here that Mia communicated her first, very big "No" of the day. My education told me better than to listen to her cries and calls and kicking at the door, so I did my best to walk away and see if it would subside once I was out of sight. It did not, and it only got worse with her starting to rear up and put her legs over the bottom door, this was not ideal and I was running out of ideas fast.

My friend asked if it was possible to place another horse next to her, since she was kind of alone even though there were horses present, they mostly chose to stay outside and not in the shelter. I needed time to think and make a new decision, I did not want to make a hasty one. Although she was right it would have made sense to try, something inside me having known the way the horse works and how strong her willpower can be told me otherwise.

The pain killers had obviously taken their effect, and with adrenaline in her system she was not showing any sign of giving up. I hastily called the vet who by that time had left and asked her if she thought it would be a ridiculous idea if I placed her back with her herd in the paddock, where she would most definitely be calmer and safer. She agreed it was a smarter idea given the horse's history, so I did it. I do not expect everyone to understand my decisions, I did what I felt was right and thankfully it too had worked. She walked right past the horse that had not so long ago kicked her to the ground and made her way directly to the hay where she had probably been standing a few hours before. The situation was exhausting to say the least, and as each day passed to our delight the swelling in her leg dispersed, therefore I could reduce the medication to its minimum. Here is the most interesting part, although it seemed logical that Mia must have lost the fight, she had after all fallen and was the receiver of the final kick, the end result was rather different. To this day I have not seen the two mares so much as place an evil ear towards each other, if anything they do not seem to acknowledge each other at all.

These days although not necessarily the highest in rank, with some new and stronger princesses fighting for that place, I would not say she is below them either. Instead one might say she was acting like some sort of queen mother or great aunt, and if there is one thing you can guarantee, anytime the mares get out of hand or some of the geldings become boyishly annoying she will use her impressive presence to step in and shut them down. That is one thing that is consistent in this beautiful mare, just as it was when she was a wild foal with her siblings, from the days when she learned how to become a domesticated horse in England in a same sex herd, right through to the days we have lived in the Netherlands in a mixed sex herd, she always went back to minding her own business by eating her hay and continuing her life as though nothing had happened.

CHAPTER 10   Part I

Synergy   Together we are strong, we are one

Life was grand spending time together like regular partners
again, a gift no money can buy, but it wasn't without some
apprehension. Naturally certain questions concerned me, such as:

"What would happen if her leg did break again?"

A good solution to aid in dimming these thoughts was to simply
continue doing what we were doing, keeping her body and mind
strong and basically doing what felt right. With the support of
the vet and her loving carers I had the confidence we could
definitely do that, resulting in some memorable occasions.
Mid-summer Mia accompanied me as my teaching horse during
a three day clinic, and that autumn one of her carers participated
with her as student for seven days at another clinic. Her sharers
at this time consisted of two girls: one a kind friend and student,
and the other the same person who was to share her a few days a
week prior to her accident. Therefore a minimum of two days a
week, I entrusted her to these two people.
It was not entirely an easy decision to make when you consider
how much we had been through. The reason I became more open
to this was not for lack of money or time, it was because it was
good for this horse to be around other people and not just me. It
dawned on me the most during the time she spent away down
south to heal for that one year. They would send photos of her
surrounded by young children grooming her tail and sitting at her
feet, it all made perfect sense.

An example of this can be explained by using children and their
equine friends. If we were to ask why most children's ponies or
horses appear brave and fearless for example compared to an

older person's pony or horse, it carries some interesting facts. I believe it is because of several reasons, the main one is indeed the children themselves. Generally children do not carry an agenda and do not usually want anything from their equine friends other than to love them unconditionally. Maybe they pull on their hair a bit, jump around or over them and so forth, yet it does not matter because the equine knows the difference, that it is harmless, the attitude of the child lays down that law. Later in life young teens or practicing adults might keep the same pony or invest in another pony or a horse, and depending on their attitude and how fast their ego starts to develop, it will be determined and reflected by the nature of their equine. More often than not, by their late teens or early adult years, their current equine friend or perhaps the new one will act very differently, showing behaviours of resistance, lack of self-confidence and environmental issues.

This really is a small example, and if recognised it can help people start to think about why horses do the things they do. In return they might stop blaming the horses, and instead ask themselves whether they are creating a brave soldier or a scared one, simply because of the attitudes surrounding them. In my teachings I often hear a common story: for example, the kind of people who rode horses when they were younger had a lot of fun and great memories, and to some degree because the horses were relatively well behaved, in retrospect they feel like they have a lot of experience. Eventually due to a change in lifestyle they had to give the hobby or horse up, maybe by moving away, getting married or having children, and then later in life the opportunity to invest time into having horses in their life again returns.

Mostly this fares the wrong way because the memories they had of the equines they rode when they were younger, are nothing like the reality they find themselves dealing with today. The horses they had the pleasure of being around back then were most likely childproof, therefore people proof and to a certain extent safe, and in their current situation they find themselves dealing with the opposite. The hardest part in these situations is that all of a sudden they do not know how to handle it and will often find themselves in trouble, which soon leads to fear and in return this of course is reflected in the horse. I know this is true; I witness it on many an occasion and I have also been there myself. The successful solution for anything like this is to share information and help get these people on a good, safe and knowledgeable path. As a horse professional I see it as my duty to do my best and develop my work to the point where the people who own horses take on the responsibility of knowing more about them, no matter what style of training they choose to use. It can only make them more successful, I have yet to see it fail.

The world is shrinking around all of us each and every day, and I believe it is up to all horse owners to train and educate their horses and help them understand the dangers that they must face living in it, including things like traffic, tractors, cows, dogs and people, not to mention people with different attitudes. It is so incredibly important, it is also vital to understand that it does not matter what problems people think they might have or how helpless they feel, they need to know that with a good and positive attitude it is possible to fix or change them. The other message I wish to share is that like me, they do not have to live in fear, they do not have to ask somebody else to fetch their horse from the pasture because it terrifies them, yet at the same time feel compelled to ride that same horse in the corner of an arena every day because the horse cannot relax at the other end, worse still because someone told them they have to.
They are creating weak soldiers all around because their attitude and ego is preventing them from changing. Unfortunately these situations are the biggest cause of accidents, and it is sometimes these same people that blame the world for their problems, yet are not prepared to make any changes themselves. We cannot expect to change everybody, or inform them that there are other ways to do things. In certain parts of the world I doubt this information will ever reach them, not in my lifetime anyway. The point I would like to make, is that I am not telling you or

anyone how or what to teach your horse, but I am advising you to find a way that works and one that is fulfilling for both you, and the horse. We must not forget that horses only know what we teach them to know, and everything else they know, is simply about survival.

Come October of 2015, Mia's condition was optimal. Looking her best in years, with a shiny black coat and extremely good muscle tone, something else struck a chord which I could not quite put my finger on. She was more often than not extremely quiet, way quieter then she had ever been in the past, and sometimes you could even say she was a bit lazy and lethargic. At first I put it down to the fact that she had more people around her now, and that maybe she had become not just a brave soldier but a super badass one. Her work regime although frequent was not super difficult at that time and actually the activity is still the same today. We have short, medium and long term goals, meaning I still teach her and myself new things. I also remind her how to use her body better and in return keep mine in shape, and for as long as she and I are here, I will continue to help her be the best she can be, and help myself to be the best I can be. In a nutshell that is it, we are not going anywhere just yet and we do not need to impress anyone anymore. Aside from my studies I went out of my way to study equine nutrition, equine health and various other topics to further my education and help my horses and students. I also invested time in communicating with a horse feed supplier and nutrition specialist, and set about helping her with her energy levels that way. Nothing much changed, and to clarify she was just quiet, not sick, not depressed, not in pain, not anything, just quiet, and although she ate her hay she had a low appetite when it came to eating things like her vitamins and supplements and sometimes a juicy carrot too, this was abnormal for her to say the least.

That same month I had scheduled an appointment at the veterinary practice to x-ray and check the old fractures, and to administer her annual vaccination while she was there. I previously made a deal with Mia and the universe that we would do this every year for the rest of her life, to check and make sure things are all in good order, sooner of course if I have concerns. After a nice chat with the head vet and admiration for his colleague who had treated her earlier that year for her fall in the paddock, I proceeded to explain the situation to him and asked if we could run a blood test to check her health levels and see if anything was wrong. He agreed of course, and after collecting more information regarding her symptoms he recommended a separate test to check her for a common condition found in many horses today called Cushing's disease, also known as PPID - Pituitary Pars Intermedia Dysfunction.

The same ritual applied by me asking Mia to stand in the stock, followed by the administration of a sedative for the x-rays and so forth. Once that was complete her blood sample was taken and she was given her vaccination. Whilst in the waiting room I saw a leaflet containing information about the PPID, I picked it up and took it with me. The results of the blood test were revealed to me two days later and they confirmed she had an extremely high count for that disease. Although extremely disappointed I was also relieved to know what it was.

The symptoms for any Cushing's horse can vary, the most common being a long and curly coat that does not shed, especially in the spring, she did not show this. However she did have what we call in the equestrian world a hay belly. One could compare it to a beer belly, yet no matter what exercise regime you undertake it will not go away.

Above the eye of a horse sits a brow that dips like a hollow pocket, and as a horse gets older during the aging process it will usually become more apparent and deeper. Mia has what are called fat deposits in the brow, so if anything they look fuller compared to other fifteen year old horses. Other symptoms she did show were of course the lethargy, quietness, low appetite and a spontaneous thirst. This all became more apparent and made perfect sense after I extensively researched the disease and recognised her personal symptoms better. The disease itself is a tumour in the pituitary gland of the brain, called a pituitary adenoma, and what this does is send inappropriate signals to the body by telling it to over-secrete a stress hormone called cortisol, and it is the cortisol that causes the imbalance in the body. So there we had it, now I had to make a new decision about the steps we would take to treat her, and help her live with the annoying condition. For approximately a week I asked around for people's advice and recommendations, I concluded that after such good feedback I would try the medication route and if it did not work I would simply just stop it. The tablets rather large in size were not ideal to feed to a horse that had no appetite, so I devised a system of dissolving the tablet each day in water, and using a plastic syringe I injected it into her mouth orally. This was trouble free, and if we are talking about Mia as a whole it was also great for her to have other people do this too, preparing the syringe (which in her mind probably looked very much like a needle), and administering the medication.

In the first weeks we saw a positive change and the famous glint in her eye shone brightly once again, she was less lethargic and did not stand at the water drinker as much. I discussed the situation with her carers and they too concluded that she looked and must have felt better. After a few months I was disappointed to discover that the membranes of her eyes looked abnormally red, her gums were also redder than normal and she contracted the odd small but irritating skin infection here and there which either disappeared as fast as it arrived, or was indeed difficult to get rid of. The disease also compromises their immune system so things like cuts and infections must be treated seriously because their body cannot fight the way it should. I called the vet out one day because her body was completely covered in bumps that looked like insect bites, and she had blisters in her mouth and on her tongue. Since it was not an emergency per se, the vet could not visit until that evening, so the bumps and blisters had almost disappeared by the time she arrived, thankfully I had taken some photos on my phone to compare it to later. The vet reassured me that it was probably nothing, perhaps an allergy or sensitivity to something, and that unfortunately this kind of thing will probably happen for the rest of her life.

One day while preparing the medication it dawned on me that the vet had also said it was possible to adjust the dose, so I decided to halve it and see what effect that would have. To all of our delight the red eyes reduced and the body rashes never came back. Towards the end of the medication when it was time to order new tablets, I decided to give her a break from them to see with my own eyes what the result of that looked like. Her red eyes completely diminished and the sparkle in her eye came back permanently. At the time of writing this book she has not been back on any form of medication. I am not saying that this decision will not change, but what I am saying is that right now she is fine and I can only hope she remains just the way she is, and continues to be okay without them. I do my best to ensure she gets the optimum and appropriate vitamins and minerals which a horse with this condition needs, and I have reduced her sugar intake as much as possible. Horses with Cushing's can also be prone to things like insulin resistance; this meant making further decisions such as not putting her out to eat grass on the pasture ever again. If it was possible to let her eat grass for a few hours at a time I would do it, but I cannot afford to let her graze on grass twenty four hours a day probably ever again, the risk is too high. Therefore today she continues to spend her time very happily in her almost perfect paddock paradise with her friends, day and night.

One final story I chose to share here happened in 2016 a few months after her initial diagnosis of the brain disease. She was due a blood test to check its status, and having weaned her off the medication and seeing that she was evidently doing well, I was apprehensive about the appointment a few days before it was scheduled. I asked myself:
Why am I doing this blood test, is there a point?
Of course there was a point, it was good to know the disease's status, but my anxiety came from another place and of course

Mia felt that. Despite the previous success with the vet taking a blood sample, I still found myself nervous about doing it without the comforts of the stock. I stupidly questioned how she would react since, aside from the lethargy, she felt incredibly well and healthy. When she had accepted the needle during the last accident, I am certain that it had only been possible because the thought that she would have a problem with it had never crossed my mind, this perhaps combined with the pain and a temporary weakness in her body which also aided in her compromise. *Never ending learning right?*

Of course when the vet arrived it all led towards Mia's immediate distrust in her. The visiting doctor was somebody we had not met yet, but she did know a little about Mia, having heard the stories from her colleagues. Through no fault of her own she made the assumption that the horse would behave the same for her. I could have kicked myself afterwards, it was another situation I should have said no to sooner. As the vet approached with the needle ready to draw her blood, Mia felt my apprehension. I could see it clearly in her eyes, and within a split second she exploded into a defensive state, and quite a big one. It was then that I said very matter of fact and as calmly as I could:

"I do not want to do continue!"

The vet recognised that it was not going to be possible, not without somebody getting hurt anyway, and shared her disappointment.
Again, I asked myself afterwards:
What was I actually saying no to?
Was I saying no because of the apprehension I had beforehand?
Was I saying no because I knew that my feeling reflected onto Mia?
Was I saying no because I did not want to hassle the horse with something I was not going to treat medically?
Not for now anyway, or was I saying no, *because my horse was now trying to attack the vet?*

175

A combination of all perhaps, but for the most part I would say that my apprehension surrounding the situation instilled enough emotion for me to know that it was not going to work. We have a saying in the horse world that I have grown to learn and love, which goes something like:

Your horse can only be as smart, brave, calm, and as athletic, as YOU are.

It is such a true statement, and would have also made a nice title for this chapter. The point is that in my bid to keep learning and sharing I need to figure out a way to try and prevent this from happening again by controlling my thoughts. If for whatever reason it does happen again, I also need to figure out a way to say no sooner. The horses and my education have already taught me, and continue to teach me, to keep my inner emotions in check and to be the best example I can be for them. Naturally I can do this with other people's animals because there is less of an emotional attachment. I have helped numerous horses overcome needle phobia to the point where the problem was permanently eliminated.

With Mia I have learned to accept that it cannot happen overnight. I can and will make mistakes, so I must forgive myself and move on, that is actually what horses do all the time. It is of course easier said than done and this is our final challenge in our life together, or maybe not. I have been asked in the past if we wanted help in these situations, such as having more people around to hold on to her. As I hope you can imagine I said no to that immediately. I have also tried having a different person hold her instead of me, this created a worse situation and a bigger fight reaction. I have practiced needle preparation using psychology in at least six different ways, including some of the old common cowboy methods. Of course they all worked because it was me doing it, but when it comes to other people it is hard to get them to use the same technique or to have the correct attitude, and for them not to be afraid when she intimidates them, it is a big ask. I am very aware that there are other ways to help both myself and Mia that we have not discovered yet. Maybe one day via somebody we trust, we will get to the bottom of this. However, my one valid excuse is that since she is a flight animal, the responses she would have to go through in order to make that choice could result in a lot of athletic movement, and one of those movements may well set her back too hard on the old fracture, I am not sure it would be worth it.

This additional pathway in Mia's journey helped create this chapter, I wanted to share it too since there are hundreds of thousands of horse owners out there in the world facing similar challenges. I also hope my experiences will help people realise that yes, although medication is not always perceived as a good thing it is not a bad thing either, it just depends on the situation. Everything is worth a try, and as far as Mia is concerned we did try it. Her condition although not life threatening at this stage, will eventually deteriorate and I will re-assess the situation as and when it happens. For now we are just incredibly grateful that she is still here, and continue to recognise how fortunate we are to be a part of her life. A professor in her own right, she is not just my teacher now, she is also yours. Her strength, willpower and majestic energy must be acknowledged, and despite all of the obstacles and provocations thrown our way I am certain of one reason that Mia is still here, and that is to share knowledge.

Over the years we have been privileged to learn from the highest calibre of equine instructors available today, they are so dedicated and have sacrificed everything, including their own private lives to learn and teach the knowledge of the horses. It is because of them, and not forgetting those surrounding us in everyday life, that I can share this story today.

Because together we are strong; together we are one, and this is called synergy.

Synergy: two or more individuals, organisations or other subjects, interacting together to create a greater effect than a solo one.

CHAPTER 10 Part II

The gift   <small>An intimate conclusion, be the leader or your life</small>

Yesterday is history, tomorrow is a mystery and today is a gift.

When I look back, the feeling associated carries some form of nostalgia, as though it was one big dream, as though it was not our experience, but somebody else's. Despite the troubles, the bullying, the trauma and the indescribable feeling of torment, to then come on out the other side the way we have, I would not change a thing; it has made us strong. Today the quality of both of our lives is probably better than it has ever been. There are two handfuls of people in our life now that I trust would take care of her perfectly should I not be able to, and there are now three people taking care of her at least one day a week, each to replace me. If you reminisce on our past, this in itself is a gift to be able to do that. The girls are all completely different in character and experience, and each and every encounter they have with Mia is simply a reflection of who they are that day. I can only admire their empathy, trust and openness for such a big responsibility, and to not just accept Mia the way she is but also allowing Mia the time to accept them.

Mia has boundaries for sure, without fault she has her rules and sticks to them; this makes her skin thick, her heart strong and her willpower endless. Ten years ago when I finally opened my heart and started to listen to hers it changed my life from the onset, and since then she continues to teach me and her girls countless things yet to be comprehended. You see in the end it is not about the horse, it is also not about the surfboard and the waves, the racing car and the speed, the parachute and the jump, the yoga and the meditation, the charity and the volunteer, the surgeon

179

and his knife, the lawyer and his win, it is about who we become when we do something we love, plus the drive and the passion we feel when we are doing it, and most importantly who we become after we have done something that matters.

It was around August of 2015 when I started to get a nagging and consistent pain in my lower back, mostly when I stood up or sat down in the same position for two long. Worse still, it also happened when I rode a horse. Approaching the age of forty years old I ignorantly pushed it to the back of my mind thinking it was something related to that, how silly. When December arrived I was in sincere agony and finally sought professional help, where an x-ray concluded Spondylosis in the L1 and L2 vertebrae. This is basically arthritis in the lower spine and the reason it hurt so bad was because it was extremely inflamed, probably due to a trauma I had not been aware of. I was advised that if I strengthened my core and back muscles to the point where I was moderately athletic it would be sustainable, and with a bit of luck I would not notice much pain. The negative news was that if I was to fall from a horse or have trauma in that area again, the pain would be more disabling next time and take longer to get better, if at all.

In my efforts to get stronger I took up swimming, unfortunately my back froze up during mid-breaststroke resulting in a further injury of a torn muscle in my right shoulder. I continued to battle forwards and saw little change for quite some time. Some obstacles included not being able to teach full time, which after a while meant little or no income. I could not work with my own horses the way I wanted to, therefore my passion was incapacitated. Things like sitting at a desk with a computer or a laptop was near impossible, so this book I had started to write was delayed. It took about four months of professional help, hard work and self-motivation before it showed any sign of getting better and stronger. As the doctor had predicted, I could start to stand for prolonged periods and without substantial pain. I could also start to work on a regular basis and do things with my own horses again. However it was all incredibly slow, and temporarily it took my spirits with it. Around May of 2016 my head started to go back to that place again, the place where I felt no good, alone, useless! And then it happened: I asked myself quite literally out loud

"What are you doing, and why are we here again Zoe?"

With all of these experiences combined and the support of my ever loving husband, family and my best friend from England, I quickly started to get back on my feet. I am dead certain that if it were not for the horses it would have been so much more difficult. They helped me snap out of it, they helped me realise each and every day that in order to get the best out of them I had to find the best in me first, especially Mia. A few times when I was strong enough to work with her in that period, she was often what you might recognise as uncooperative or naughty. My feeling so low I only saw the worst in the situation, leading me to feel sorry for myself even more. For a while there it was a bit of a mess, and although nothing was as ugly and illuminated as it had been in the past, she reminded me quickly who she was ten years ago by running around like a headless chicken, showing a lack of self-confidence and high concern for her environment. What she in fact did do was show me who I was in the past, and who I was in that very moment and it was somebody neither I nor Mia wanted me to be. She was my reflection and I had to change that.

Through the horses I know who I am now.
They live in the moment not in the past.
NOT the past.

When I first considered writing this book, I hesitated and dithered for months and months and procrastinated to the point where I let my fears take over. One day when the temptation was close and I could not stand the itch inside me anymore, I asked myself: *what are you afraid of?*

181

Shrugging my shoulders I pushed any apprehension aside, put pen to paper and started to write. I did not have to use my imagination to create this story, it was already there, the hard part was figuring out how to tell it.

One of the first proof readers who is a regular carer of Mia wrote in her notes:

"She turned her can't into can and her dream into a plan!"

That is exactly what I wanted this book to represent; a story of dreams, a story of realities, a story about how to be the leader of *YOUR* life.

I know now that life is one big lesson and you can either choose to embrace it or ignore it, I embrace it.
If I put one foot in front of the other, work hard and offer solutions instead of complaints my world is already a much nicer place.
If I refuse to let fear stop me from doing what I want to do, I am free.
If I allow the opinions of others to falter my dreams, and that includes the writing of this book, I am not in control of my life.
With that said, we must have boundaries; we cannot expect our horses or even our children to have them if we do not.
Just like humans no two horses are alike, and if we understand them first, the way they think, act and feel, we will be much more successful in their presence. Therefore I encourage everybody that is interested in them to really go and learn about them, because trust me they already know everything they need to know about you.

I also know that I thrive when I am busy, so I will keep doing so. I like to keep my promises and let people know when I cannot, even if it is later than they might like. I like to educate and inspire and I like to help people be the best they can be for themselves, their loved ones and their horses. I am confident now when I say I have little time for pointless small talk, peer pressure, jealousy and big egos. What people say or think about me, really is none of my business. Sometimes when things feel as though they have lost their perspective, or life takes a natural course of imbalance I am allowed to struggle, it is just the way I am. Learning how to just go with the flow, to not worry about the small stuff and keep on smiling when things do not necessarily go the way I want is hard for everybody. I am not a victim, I am just me, and me is good enough.

In closing I can tell you that Mia's health is stable, and we are in no hurry for anything anymore. We have probably learned to understand more than most that it takes time for the body to heal, and that includes broken bones. I promise to do my best for her, for you, and most importantly for me. I will never pretend I can do something that I cannot, or pretend I am something I am not, *because do you know what will happen if I do?*

Mia, my (our) idol, will be the first to let us know!

> **Idol:** a person or thing that is greatly admired, loved and/or remembered – hero, heroine, superstar, icon.

CHAPTER 11

The journals   A record of past accounts

Diary entries recorded since 2007, of moments spontaneously selected from my records:

5th October 2007
In just under half a year our progress is huge. I cannot believe how much I can see now, compared to quite possibly my whole life before. Although it can be mentally demanding, it is positive. I must keep focusing forwards. When things go a bit wrong, she is a lot of horse but these moments are so much shorter, she seems *smaller* in her efforts. I am excited. The future moments are only breaths we have not taken yet, and I will keep working hard to make sure they become pure oxygen. I cannot wait!

5th February 2008
The concept of looking forwards and not backwards has paid off immensely. We have crossed so many borders, ones I hope never to return to and if we do, I will certainly know better how to handle them. Her self-confidence (and mine) continues to grow. In situations she happens to be unconfident I am getting better at helping her, by seeing and respecting her thresholds or by moving on, and quicker than ever before.

21st May 2008
I have been busy preparing for our wedding but have done my best to not lose focus as far as Mia is concerned! The main areas of improvement have been my not worrying about old things and moving on with the new. Everything we do together is almost effortless. My only struggle now during our sessions is knowing how long to continue and how soon to quit. I also understand that

the end of today will set me up for tomorrow. If our progress remains stable like this, I (we) will be forever happy. What a journey so far, very proud.

22nd July 2008
Thirty minutes of time doing nothing together again today, I love these moments as apparently does she. She has started to really open up and I am in awe of her suggestions. Wow, just WOW.

6th August 2008
Some BIG lessons today - in my willingness to progress I have sacrificed some things. Her expression has become a bit dull and sometimes even angry. I need to slow right down and re-evaluate our training. I need to right these wrongs. Other than this we are becoming a good team and I am so very proud of everything. There IS so much more to learn yet, I must be patient. I must also forgive myself for my mistakes and move on. I am sure she will continue to help with that, I am listening.

27th March 2009
Patience and persistence have continued to pay off again. I do not recognise us anymore and only in a good way. I noticed that my confidence in riding is not quite there yet, well not as high as it is when working on the ground anyway. The difference now is I feel as though she is helping me to do this and is acting like a real partner, I can't quite believe it. I have some new study material to get on with, it is perfectly timed. Love you Mia.

10th September 2009
I had the opportunity to work on trailer loading with excellence again today. Since she never really had issues with loading when it was her idea, I did notice a few questions when it was my idea, especially when I want to go somewhere. Some old habits showed up like her rearing, but I hung in there. She now loads straight at trot and comes back out straight too, and only when I ask. All the pieces of this puzzle are coming together and make perfect sense.

2nd January 2010

I am so excited, heading to the USA to attend an official course. I am also quite nervous, apparently Mia felt that today when I rode her, so I got off and worked with her from the ground instead. I love the reverse information this education offers, why stay on if your brain tells you to get off? Whereas tradition tells you to stay on! Usually that is when accidents happen. Prevention is better than cure and everybody is the winner.

17th September 2010

Have just returned from the USA after three intense months of training and am now officially qualified to teach. There are no words to describe my excitement and what the future has to offer. I will give it 100% and if that is not enough I am sure I can find in me much more. Onwards and upwards!

7th July 2011

Made it to England!! What a looooooooooooooooooong day! Things worked against me a bit, having had traffic in Belgium, France and then all around London. I think this added a total of five hours extra journey time. Mia was a trooper and did not complain once. I felt nervous leaving her on her own on the boat, but had no choice. As soon as I got upstairs I found a chair and grabbed some sleep, I'm glad I did. I met mum and dad as we passed by home for a quick hello and a snack, it was fun. I am excited for the next two weeks being home again with Mia and learning directly from the source.

10th August 2011

It was a busy day again today so I had a quick liberty session with Mia. Knowing I had minimal time I told myself to pretend we had all day and lived in the moment so to speak. We got some great things going with a good energy and solid transitions! Fabulous :)

14th November 2011

I rode Mia for the first time in the new saddle, WOW! She felt great, forward and relaxed. I rode around at first in trot for about 20 minutes. She felt so comfortable she really wanted to move forwards, I think the other saddle must have been hurting somewhere because she did quit moving when I quit riding, no biggy, it took some time and I had to find a new connection because of it!! Very interesting!!

4th April 2012

We rode for only ten minutes today, I asked for a collected canter, she blew me away, what a feeling. After 5-8 strides of this, I just quit riding, she came to a halt, I threw the reins on her neck, jumped off and with a huge grin, I said: "That was it girl, THANK YOU XXX"

30th July 2012

Great session today!! I started on the ground to check some things out and then rode. These days I always try to start with a nice loose walk, trot and canter as much as possible until she really starts to relax. No more ears back in the walk to canter transitions. I worked out that I was doing too much again and also that she did not quite understand the aid. Solved :-) Back up is getting better and for longer distances. Canter to stop also felt good today, all of this without using the reins. We finished with some lateral work and we manged to do two flying changes. She had problems relaxing afterwards, so we will work on that. Love it all, love her.

20th November 2012

I could feel her energy the moment I met her today and it was high, so I decided to visit a place we have not been for a while and worked with her in the round pen. She was insanely full of energy, so I let her have her idea until she was ready to have mine. She had a blast and must have felt much better after a good gallop. On days like this I will just go with it, crazy horse ;-)

19th May 2013

I had a lovely and unquestionable ride in the dunes with a friend, I miss those days, a shame really, we used to do this much more often. Mia was relaxed and soft, even when we saw the cows. She questioned them as always, but that is just her and she was over it in seconds. I barely used the reins too, that is BIG!

17th June 2013

Today my heart broke clean in two along with her knee fracture. I can't quite believe what the vet has told me. He will call me tomorrow with a conclusion as to what we can do. I hope and pray it does not mean I have lost her, I cannot bear the thought.

2nd August 2013

Sometimes the human species embarrasses me. I have no words to describe the torment of some people, they are relentless in what I believe is an ambition to make me feel bad or wrong. I am currently searching for a place to take her after her next check-up where she can live in quiet and we can both have some peace of mind.

3rd March 2014

I visited Mia again this weekend and she is doing very well. One of the donkeys seems to have fallen in love with her, I can almost see the love hearts fly above his head.

2nd November 2014

I still cannot quite believe she is home and has been able to do things again. The future looks promising, although I am confident when I say I am prepared if something changes. She is so strong, I need to continue to be so too.

1st December 2014

She is feeling good but has trouble sometimes to fully relax in her left shoulder. We have a massage scheduled on Saturday so this should help answer some questions. ☺

6th February 2015

In hindsight, this is a horse that used to run away from my leg when riding, not forgetting to mention she would bolt, buck and spook. After breaking two legs I am so grateful we can do the things we do. Today is one example of why I love doing what I do and want to learn more and more. I asked for 10 minutes of trot each way on a loose rein. No hassle, nice tempo, no falling on the forehand and no running away mentally or emotionally.... Awesome :-)

22nd June 2015

Today my goal was to ride and work on areas we need to progress so that we can move to the next level, and help her posture and health even more than I have been doing so far. I have booked an appointment with an osteopath, it is time :-)

19th November 2015

It was nice to be back again after a week away in Malta. I rode Kheelen and took Mia with us on line for a ride in the dunes again. I love the nature and the peace and quiet. The horses work great together like this. It got me thinking that maybe I should seriously think about writing a book to tell Mia's story.

11th February 2016

Still not able to do much because of my back and shoulder! Very disappointed, I feel disabled and I am starting to feel a bit down about it all, I need to find a way to lift my spirits again, and need to make some new plans. Both horses are doing OK, which is all that matters.

13th August 2016

I am heading to the USA next week, yippeee! The care schedule for both horses is almost final, and I am looking forward to mine and Jort's ventures away. I decided to give both horses a vacation while I am gone; they both deserve it, especially my old chum, Mia.

CHAPTER 12

The Equus   A poem dedicated to the Equus

Choice and a destiny, something on their mind,
the usual resolution or a prisoner confined.
Snow, rain or thunder, shut in, cannot be outside,
trapped and frightened, or man whipping at their side.

Angelic and innocent, things not easily forgot,
comfortable living or their soul and mind left to rot.
Fear and mechanics, broke their beauty for many years,
if dare resist, only hit harder, confirming their fears.

A servant and companion for mankind all these centuries,
yet subject to relentless cruelty, like the land, sea and trees.
Stop, look and listen, what are they trying to say,
perhaps a simple promise of safety, comfort, food and play.

There are a special few, who listen to their souls,
understanding their nature as adults and young foals.
A promise of a language, both can try to understand,
no punishment required, a mutual respect of a command.

Time is all that is needed, to get things good and right,
or the same thing is done over and over, resulting in a fight.
Look at their ears, in their eyes, hear them breathe and sigh,
man has started to change their method and ask how and why.

They have survived the ice age, roamed our earth for so long,
a question of what we love about them, where did it all go wrong.
A chief would ride in full gallop, shooting arrows from their back,
how was this possible in the open prairie, no whip, spur or tack.

Caring for the young, not taken from their mother too soon,
in nature's elements on the land, under the sun, stars and moon.
Some cowboys, they did their best, others sacrificed their health,
by selling their dignity and soul, to entertain their own wealth.

Cavalry and order, corruption, war and theft,
a new rule, when training you must do everything on the left.
For years this was the law, the only way it should be done,
a chief's prayer has been reborn, mother nature has won.

If possible, perhaps the horses would smile and be joyous,
man has found the old path to return their dignity, little fuss.
Majestic and innocent, yet so fragile our friend the Equus,
a servant of the earth, a living being and a right to EQUAL US.

You are invited to visit this book's companion website and social media page for images, videos and updates:

www.thehorsethatbroketwolegs.com
www.facebook.com/thehorsethatbroketwolegs

Printed in Great Britain
by Amazon